The Complete Crock Pot Cookbook for Beginners

2000+ Days of Delicious & Super Easy Slow Cooker Recipes with Simple Ingredients, Plus an Easy-to-Follow 30-Day Meal Plan for Effortless Cooking and Enjoyment

Savor Wholesome Flavors with Every Slow-Cooked Meal

Levi Reeds

TABLE OF CONTENTS

INTRODUCTION

Dear readers,

Levi Reeds, a seasoned culinary expert and advocate for effortless, healthy cooking, brings his extensive knowledge of slow cooker recipes to his latest work. With a deep passion for creating nutritious and flavorful meals, Levi has mastered the art of utilizing the Crock Pot, making healthy eating accessible and enjoyable for everyone.

His approach to cooking seamlessly blends simplicity and sophistication, ensuring each recipe is easy to prepare while packed with vibrant flavors and wholesome ingredients. Levi's commitment to promoting a balanced diet without sacrificing taste is evident throughout his comprehensive cookbook.

Levi's journey into slow cooking is both professional and personal. Having experienced the transformative power of meal planning and easy-to-follow recipes, he understands the challenges beginners face when adopting new cooking methods. This empathy drives his mission to empower others to embrace slow cooking as a way to achieve their health and lifestyle goals effortlessly.

Levi offers over 100 delicious and super easy slow cooker recipes, each crafted with simple ingredients to cater to various tastes and dietary needs. The book also features a meticulously designed 30-day meal plan, providing readers with a structured yet flexible roadmap to streamline their cooking process and enhance their culinary experience.

Beyond recipes, Levi provides invaluable tips on meal prepping, ingredient substitutions, and maximizing the Crock Pot's functionality to save time and reduce kitchen stress. His goal is to make the journey toward healthier living not only achievable but also enjoyable and sustainable.

CHAPTER 1: UNDERSTANDING THE CROCK POT DIET

The Benefits of Slow Cooking

Embracing the Crock Pot Diet means tapping into the incredible advantages that slow cooking offers for both your health and your lifestyle. As a seasoned chef and a dedicated advocate for healthy eating, I've witnessed firsthand how the humble slow cooker can transform everyday meals into nourishing, flavorful masterpieces. Let's explore the myriad benefits of slow cooking and how it can enhance your journey toward a healthier you.

1. Nutrient Preservation

One of the standout benefits of slow cooking is its ability to preserve the essential nutrients in your ingredients. Unlike high-heat cooking methods that can degrade vitamins and minerals, slow cooking operates at lower temperatures over extended periods. This gentle process helps retain vital nutrients such as vitamins B and C, antioxidants, and minerals like potassium and magnesium. As a result, your meals are not only delicious but also packed with the nutrients your body needs to thrive.

2. Enhanced Flavor and Tenderness

Slow cooking excels at developing deep, rich flavors that are often unattainable through quick cooking methods. The extended cooking time allows herbs, spices, and other seasonings to meld seamlessly with your ingredients, creating a harmonious blend of tastes. Additionally, tougher cuts of meat become irresistibly tender as the slow cooker breaks down connective tissues, resulting in succulent, melt-in-your-mouth dishes. This flavor enhancement means you can enjoy hearty, satisfying meals without the need for excessive fats or salts.

3. Convenience and Time-Saving

In our fast-paced lives, finding the time to prepare healthy meals can be challenging. The Crock Pot Diet offers unparalleled convenience, allowing you to set up your ingredients in the morning and return to a fully cooked meal in the evening. This hands-off approach not only saves time but also reduces the stress of daily meal preparation. With minimal effort required, you can maintain a consistent, healthy eating routine without sacrificing your busy schedule.

4. Portion Control and Weight Management

Slow cooking encourages the use of whole, unprocessed ingredients, which are naturally lower in calories and higher in nutrients compared to many store-bought alternatives. By controlling the ingredients and their quantities, you can easily manage portion sizes and caloric intake, supporting your weight management goals. Additionally, slow-cooked meals are often more filling due to their high fiber and protein content, helping you feel satisfied longer and reducing the likelihood of unhealthy snacking.

5. Versatility and Meal Variety

The slow cooker is an incredibly versatile kitchen tool that can handle a wide array of recipes, from soups and stews to casseroles and desserts. This versatility ensures that your Crock Pot Diet remains exciting and diverse, preventing the monotony that can sometimes accompany diet plans. Whether you're craving a comforting beef stew, a vibrant vegetable curry, or a sweet apple crisp, the slow cooker can accommodate your culinary desires with ease.

6. Cost-Effective Cooking

Eating healthy doesn't have to break the bank. Slow cooking often utilizes more affordable cuts of meat and seasonal vegetables, making it a budget-friendly option for nutritious meals. The ability to prepare large batches also means you can enjoy leftovers throughout the week, further stretching your food budget. By minimizing food waste and maximizing ingredient usage, the Crock Pot Diet offers both financial and nutritional benefits.

7. Improved Digestion and Metabolic Health

Slow-cooked meals are typically easier to digest, as the extended cooking process breaks down complex carbohydrates and proteins into simpler forms. This can be particularly beneficial for individuals with digestive sensitivities or those looking to improve their overall gut health. Additionally, the emphasis on whole foods and balanced meals supports metabolic health, helping to regulate blood sugar levels and reduce the risk of chronic diseases such as diabetes and heart disease.

8. Stress Reduction and Mindful Eating

Preparing meals in a slow cooker encourages a more mindful approach to eating. With the majority of the cooking process handled by the appliance, you can focus on other aspects of your day, reducing the stress associated with meal planning and preparation. This relaxed cooking environment fosters a positive relationship with food, allowing you to savor each meal without the pressure of time constraints.

How the Crock Pot Diet Enhances Nutrition

Adopting the Crock Pot Diet is not just a shift in your cooking routine—it's a transformative approach to nourishing your body with wholesome, nutrient-dense meals. As both a professional chef and a specialist in the Crock Pot Diet, I've seen firsthand how slow cooking can elevate the nutritional profile of your meals, supporting overall health and well-being. Let's delve into the specific ways the Crock Pot Diet enhances nutrition and why it's a superior choice for those seeking a balanced, health-conscious lifestyle.

1. Preservation of Essential Nutrients

One of the most significant nutritional benefits of slow cooking is the preservation of essential vitamins and minerals. Unlike high-heat cooking methods such as frying or grilling, slow cooking operates at lower temperatures over extended periods. This gentle process helps retain heat-sensitive nutrients like vitamin C, B vitamins, and antioxidants that are often lost during rapid cooking. Additionally, the extended cooking time allows flavors to meld without the need for excessive salt or unhealthy fats, ensuring your meals remain both nutritious and delicious.

2. Enhanced Bioavailability of Nutrients

Slow cooking not only preserves nutrients but can also enhance their bioavailability—the ease with which your body can absorb and utilize them. For example, cooking vegetables like tomatoes and spinach in a slow cooker breaks down their cellular structures, making it easier for your body to absorb beneficial compounds such as lycopene and iron. This means that the nutrients in your slow-cooked meals are more readily available to support your body's functions, from boosting your immune system to improving energy levels.

3. Balanced and Complete Meals

The Crock Pot Diet encourages the use of a variety of whole foods, including lean proteins, whole grains, and an abundance of vegetables. This focus on diversity ensures that each meal is nutritionally balanced, providing a comprehensive array of macronutrients (proteins, fats, and carbohydrates) and micronutrients (vitamins and minerals). By combining different food groups in a single dish, the Crock Pot Diet promotes a well-rounded diet that supports muscle growth, brain function, and overall cellular health.

4. Controlled Use of Ingredients

One of the keys to the Crock Pot Diet's nutritional superiority is the ability to control the quality and quantity of ingredients used. When preparing meals in a slow cooker, you have full oversight of what goes into your dishes, allowing you to minimize the use of processed ingredients, added sugars, and unhealthy fats. This level of control ensures that your meals are tailored to your specific dietary needs and health goals, whether you're aiming to reduce sodium intake, increase fiber consumption, or incorporate more plant-based proteins into your diet.

5. Reduction of Harmful Compounds

High-heat cooking methods can produce harmful compounds such as advanced glycation end products (AGEs) and heterocyclic amines (HCAs), which have been linked to various health issues, including inflammation and cancer. Slow cooking significantly reduces the formation of these harmful substances by cooking food at lower temperatures. This makes the Crock Pot Diet a safer option for regular meal preparation, minimizing your exposure to potentially dangerous compounds while still delivering flavorful and satisfying meals.

6. Emphasis on Whole, Unprocessed Foods

The Crock Pot Diet inherently promotes the consumption of whole, unprocessed foods. By focusing on fresh vegetables, lean meats, whole grains, and natural herbs and spices, this diet minimizes the intake of preservatives, artificial additives, and refined sugars commonly found in processed foods. Whole foods are rich in essential nutrients and free from the empty calories that can contribute to weight gain and other health problems, making them the cornerstone of a nutritious and sustainable diet.

7. Supports Digestive Health

Slow-cooked meals are typically easier to digest compared to their quickly prepared counterparts. The prolonged cooking process breaks down complex fibers and proteins, reducing the strain on your digestive system. This can be particularly beneficial for individuals with digestive sensitivities or those looking to improve gut health. A healthy digestive system is crucial for the absorption of nutrients and the elimination of toxins, both of which are essential for maintaining overall health and preventing chronic diseases.

8. Facilitates Weight Management

The Crock Pot Diet supports weight management through its emphasis on nutrient-dense, low-calorie meals that are high in fiber and protein. High-fiber foods promote satiety, helping you feel fuller for longer periods and reducing the likelihood of overeating. Additionally, lean proteins help build and maintain muscle mass, which is essential for a healthy metabolism. By providing balanced meals that satisfy hunger without excess calories, the Crock Pot Diet makes it easier to achieve and maintain a healthy weight.

9. Encourages Mindful Eating

Slow cooking fosters a more mindful approach to eating. With the majority of the cooking process handled by the slow cooker, you can focus on preparing quality ingredients and enjoying the process of creating nourishing meals. This mindfulness extends to your eating habits, encouraging you to savor each bite and pay attention to your body's hunger and fullness cues. Mindful eating is a powerful tool for improving your relationship with food, enhancing digestion, and promoting long-term dietary success.

10. Supports Sustainable Eating Practices

The Crock Pot Diet aligns with sustainable eating practices by emphasizing the use of seasonal, locally sourced ingredients and minimizing food waste. Slow cookers are ideal for cooking large batches of food, allowing you to enjoy leftovers and reduce the frequency of grocery shopping trips. This not only saves time and money but also contributes to a more sustainable lifestyle by making efficient use of resources and supporting local agriculture.

Key Ingredients for Crock Pot Cooking

Embarking on the Crock Pot Diet journey requires not only the right mindset but also a well-stocked pantry filled with versatile, nutritious ingredients. As a professional chef and specialist in the Crock Pot Diet, I understand the importance of selecting the best ingredients to maximize the health benefits and flavors of your slow-cooked meals. This section highlights the essential categories and specific ingredients that will elevate your Crock Pot creations, ensuring your meals are both delicious and nutritionally balanced.

1. Lean Proteins

Protein is a cornerstone of any healthy diet, essential for muscle repair, immune function, and overall cellular health. Slow cooking is particularly effective for tenderizing lean cuts of meat, making them flavorful and succulent without the need for excessive fats.

- **Chicken Breast and Thighs:** Versatile and easy to prepare, chicken thighs are slightly fattier than breasts, adding richness to dishes without compromising health.
- **Turkey:** Ground turkey or turkey breast provides a lean alternative to red meats, perfect for a variety of recipes from stews to casseroles.
- **Beef Chuck and Brisket:** These tougher cuts become melt-in-your-mouth tender when slow-cooked, absorbing flavors beautifully.
- **Pork Tenderloin and Shoulder:** Lean yet flavorful, pork shoulder is ideal for pulled pork recipes, while tenderloin offers a leaner option.
- **Fish and Seafood:** While not all fish are suitable for long cooking times, sturdy varieties like salmon and cod thrive in the

Crock Pot, maintaining their moisture and nutrients.

2. Whole Grains

Incorporating whole grains into your Crock Pot meals adds fiber, vitamins, and minerals, promoting digestive health and sustained energy levels.

- **Quinoa:** A complete protein, quinoa cooks relatively quickly in the slow cooker and absorbs surrounding flavors well.
- **Brown Rice and Wild Rice:** These grains offer a hearty texture and nutty flavor, perfect for pilafs and rice-based casseroles.
- **Farro:** With its chewy texture and nutty taste, farro is excellent in salads and hearty soups.
- **Barley:** Barley adds a wonderful texture to soups and stews, providing essential fiber and nutrients.
- **Oats:** Steel-cut or rolled oats can be used for breakfast porridges or as a thickening agent in soups.

3. Legumes and Pulses

Legumes are nutrient-dense, high in protein and fiber, making them an excellent addition to the Crock Pot Diet. They support heart health, stabilize blood sugar, and promote satiety.

- **Lentils:** Quick-cooking and versatile, lentils are perfect for soups, stews, and salads.
- **Black Beans and Kidney Beans:** These beans add hearty texture and robust flavor to chili, casseroles, and rice dishes.
- **Chickpeas:** Ideal for curries, stews, and Mediterranean-inspired dishes, chickpeas bring a creamy texture when slow-cooked.
- **Split Peas:** Perfect for comforting soups and stews, split peas break down to create a thick, satisfying texture.

4. Fresh and Root Vegetables

Vegetables are packed with essential vitamins, minerals, and antioxidants. Selecting the right vegetables ensures your meals are colorful, nutritious, and flavorful.

- **Carrots and Potatoes:** These staples add sweetness and heartiness to soups, stews, and roasts.
- **Onions and Garlic:** Essential aromatics that form the flavor base for countless dishes.
- **Bell Peppers and Zucchini:** These versatile vegetables cook quickly and add vibrant color and texture to your meals.
- **Broccoli and Cauliflower:** Perfect for adding bulk and nutrients to casseroles and vegetable medleys.
- **Sweet Potatoes and Butternut Squash:** These root vegetables offer natural sweetness and a creamy texture when slow-cooked.

5. Fresh Herbs and Spices

Enhancing your dishes with the right herbs and spices elevates the flavor without adding unnecessary calories or sodium. They also offer various health benefits, including anti-inflammatory and antioxidant properties.

- **Thyme and Rosemary:** These robust herbs are perfect for hearty stews and roasts.
- **Basil and Oregano:** Ideal for Italian and Mediterranean-inspired dishes, adding fresh, aromatic notes.
- **Cumin and Coriander:** Essential for adding warmth and depth to chili, curries, and Mexican dishes.
- **Paprika and Chili Powder:** Perfect for adding smoky and spicy flavors to soups, stews, and meat dishes.
- **Ginger and Turmeric:** These spices provide a subtle heat and offer powerful anti-inflammatory benefits, great for Asian-inspired recipes.

6. Healthy Fats

Incorporating healthy fats into your Crock Pot meals supports heart health, aids in nutrient absorption, and adds richness to your dishes.

- **Olive Oil:** A staple in Mediterranean cooking, olive oil adds depth and flavor while providing monounsaturated fats.
- **Coconut Oil:** Ideal for adding a subtle sweetness and creaminess to curries and stews.
- **Avocado:** Perfect for garnishing and adding creaminess to salads and soups after cooking.
- **Nuts and Seeds:** Almonds, walnuts, and sunflower seeds can add crunch and additional nutrients to salads and casseroles.

7. Broths and Stocks

Using quality broths and stocks as the cooking liquid enhances the flavor and nutritional value of your dishes. Opt for low-sodium versions to control salt intake.

- **Chicken Broth:** Versatile and rich in flavor, perfect for a wide range of recipes.
- **Beef Broth:** Adds depth to hearty stews and meat-based dishes.
- **Vegetable Broth:** Ideal for vegetarian and vegan recipes, providing a robust base without animal products.
- **Bone Broth:** Packed with collagen and minerals, bone broth supports joint and skin health, adding a nutritious boost to soups and stews.

8. Dairy and Alternatives

Dairy adds creaminess and richness to your dishes, while alternatives cater to various dietary preferences and restrictions.

- **Greek Yogurt:** Adds tanginess and creaminess to sauces and dressings when added after cooking.
- **Cheese:** Mozzarella, Parmesan, and cheddar add flavor and texture to casseroles and baked dishes.
- **Coconut Milk:** Perfect for creamy curries and soups, adding a rich texture without dairy.
- **Plant-Based Milks:** Almond, soy, and oat milks can be used as substitutes in various recipes for those with lactose intolerance or following a vegan diet.

9. Whole Foods and Minimally Processed Ingredients

Focusing on whole, minimally processed ingredients ensures your meals are free from unnecessary additives and preservatives, aligning with the principles of the Crock Pot Diet.

- **Fresh Produce:** Always choose fresh, seasonal vegetables and fruits for maximum flavor and nutrient content.
- **Whole Grains:** Opt for whole grains over refined options to increase fiber intake and promote sustained energy levels.
- **Natural Sweeteners:** Use honey, maple syrup, or natural sweeteners in moderation to add sweetness without the drawbacks of refined sugars.
- **Lean Meats and Plant Proteins:** Prioritize lean cuts of meat and plant-based proteins to keep your meals nutritious and aligned with health goals.

10. Liquid Components for Moisture and Flavor

Ensuring adequate moisture in your slow cooker prevents drying out and enhances the flavors of your dishes. Choose liquids that complement your ingredients and contribute to the overall taste profile.

- **Tomato-Based Sauces:** Ideal for stews, chili, and casseroles, adding acidity and depth.
- **Creamy Bases:** Ingredients like coconut milk or dairy alternatives create rich, comforting textures.
- **Vinegars and Citrus Juices:** Add brightness and balance to your dishes, enhancing the overall flavor.

Tips for Selecting and Preparing Ingredients

- **Quality Matters:** Invest in high-quality, fresh ingredients to ensure the best flavors and nutritional benefits.
- **Prep Ahead:** Chop and measure your ingredients before cooking to streamline the cooking process and ensure even distribution in the slow cooker.
- **Layer Strategically:** Place harder vegetables and meats at the bottom of the Crock Pot where they receive the most heat, ensuring even cooking.

- **Avoid Overfilling:** Adhere to the manufacturer's guidelines for your slow cooker to prevent overcooking and ensure optimal results.

Conclusion

Choosing the right ingredients is pivotal to the success of the Crock Pot Diet. By focusing on lean proteins, whole grains, nutrient-dense vegetables, and a thoughtful selection of herbs and spices, you can create meals that are not only delicious but also support your health and wellness goals. Embrace these key ingredients and let your slow cooker work its magic, transforming simple components into nourishing, flavorful dishes that make healthy eating effortless and enjoyable.

CHAPTER 2: 30-DAY MEAL PLAN

Day	Breakfast (650 kcal)	Lunch (600 kcal)	Snack (300 kcal)	Dinner (350 kcal)
1	Spinach and Feta Egg Casserole – p.16	Beef and Barley Stew – p.31	Tomato Basil Bruschetta – p.45	Lemon Garlic Salmon with Quinoa Pilaf – p.66
2	Cheesy Mushroom and Herb Frittata – p.16	Chicken Noodle Soup – p.32	Greek Yogurt Spinach Dip with Veggie Sticks – p.45	Shrimp Scampi with Zucchini Noodles – p.66
3	Quiche Lorraine – p.28	Creamy Mushroom and Wild Rice Soup – p.32	Spinach Artichoke Dip with Whole Grain Lavash – p.46	Mediterranean Cod with Couscous Salad – p.67
4	Savory Oatmeal with Spinach and Poached Egg – p.21	Creamy Broccoli and Cheddar Soup – p.33	Roasted Red Pepper Hummus with Pita – p.46	Pesto Crusted Trout with Spinach and Cherry Tomatoes – p.67
5	Southwestern Egg and Sausage Breakfast Bake – p.19	Vegetable Minestrone – p.33	Avocado and Black Bean Salsa with Tortilla Chips – p.47	Tilapia with Herb Butter and Roasted Asparagus – p.68
6	Zucchini and Parmesan Egg Muffins – p.17	Butternut Squash and Red Lentil Stew – p.34	Baked Brie with Berries – p.47	Spicy Cajun Catfish with Corn on the Cob – p.68
7	Protein-Packed Veggie Omelette – p.27	Turkey and Quinoa Chili – p.34	Baked Cinnamon Apples – p.48	Chicken Pot Pie – p.69
8	Mushroom and Spinach Stuffed Peppers – p.27	Chicken and Vegetable Ragout – p.35	Lemon Blueberry Greek Yogurt Cake – p.48	Farro and Roasted Vegetable Pilaf – p.69
9	Egg Muffins with Turkey and Spinach – p.25	Mediterranean Vegetable Ragout – p.35	Lemon Chia Seed Pudding – p.49	Beef and Bean Enchiladas – p.70
10	Broccoli, Cheddar, and Salmon Breakfast Quiche – p.18	Farro and Apple Salad – p.36	Peach Yogurt Crumble – p.49	Tomato Basil Zucchini Bake – p.70
11	Egg Bake – p.17	Quinoa and Black Bean Salad – p.36	Raspberry Almond Tart – p.50	Mushroom and Spinach Lasagna – p.71
12	Turkey Sausage, Zucchini, and Egg White Casserole – p.24	Wild Rice and Cranberry Salad – p.37	Vanilla Almond Protein Balls – p.50	Mushroom and Quinoa Stuffed Zucchini – p.71
13	Cottage Cheese and Raisin Berry Casserole – p.24	Lentil and Vegetable Stew – p.37	Dark Chocolate Walnut Brownies – p.51	Classic Chicken and Vegetable Paella – p.72
14	Grilled Vegetable and Hummus Wrap – p.30	Spinach and Ricotta Stuffed Shells – p.38	Raspberry Oat Bars – p.51	Mediterranean Turkey Paella – p.72
15	Spinach and Feta Egg Casserole – p.16	Gorgonzola and Pear Risotto – p.38	Blueberry Banana Bread – p.52	Roasted Vegetable and Goat Cheese Tart – p.73
16	Egg Muffins with Turkey and Spinach – p.25	Creamy Tomato and Basil Pasta – p.39	Lemon Poppy Seed Bread – p.52	Herbed Tomato and Feta Tart – p.73
17	Lemon Blueberry French Toast Casserole – p.30	Butternut Squash and Sage Risotto – p.39	Pumpkin Spice Bread – p.53	Ratatouille – p.59
18	Savory Amaranth with Bacon and Leeks – p.22	Beef Stroganoff with Whole-Grain Noodles – p.40	Raspberry White Chocolate Bread – p.53	Vegetable Lasagna – p.59
19	Farro Breakfast Bowl with Roasted Vegetables – p.21	Honey Garlic Chicken with Quinoa – p.40	Pecan Pie Bars – p.54	Zucchini and Tomato Gratin – p.60

Day	Breakfast (650 kcal)	Lunch (600 kcal)	Snack (300 kcal)	Dinner (350 kcal)
20	Cottage Cheese and Raisin Berry Casserole – p.24	Pork Tenderloin with Apples and Wild Rice – p.41	Keto Bagels – p.54	Savory Mushroom and Spinach Bake – p.60
21	Spinach and Feta Stuffed Peppers – p.27	BBQ Pulled Chicken with Brown Rice – p.41	Almond Butter Blondies – p.55	Roasted Broccoli with Cauliflower and Cheese – p.61
22	Spinach and Feta Egg Casserole – p.16	Beef and Sweet Potato Shepherd's Pie – p.42	Cheddar Biscuits – p.55	Stuffed Mushrooms – p.61
23	Savory Oatmeal with Spinach and Poached Egg – p.21	Slow-Roasted Herb Chicken with Root Vegetables – p.42	Lemon Poppy Seed Muffins – p.56	Warm Barley and Roasted Vegetable Salad – p.62
24	Protein-Packed Veggie Omelette – p.27	Italian Meatballs in Marinara Sauce with Orzo and Spinach – p.43	Lemon Cheesecake – p.56	Black Bean and Corn Salad – p.62
25	Spinach and Feta Egg Casserole – p.16	Beef and Vegetable Kebabs with Quinoa – p.44	Pineapple Upside Down Cake – p.57	Warm Beet and Goat Cheese Salad – p.63
26	Cheesy Mushroom and Herb Frittata – p.16	Beef and Broccoli with Brown Rice – p.44	Caramel Apple Dump Cake – p.58	Spinach and Mushroom Salad with Balsamic Vinaigrette – p.63
27	Eggplant Parmesan – p.28	Honey Garlic Chicken with Quinoa – p.40	Mango Coconut Rice Pudding – p.58	Quinoa and Kale Salad – p.64
28	Zucchini and Parmesan Egg Muffins – p.17	Beef Stroganoff with Whole-Grain Noodles – p.40	Baked Cinnamon Apples – p.48	Broccoli and Cranberry Salad – p.64
29	Egg Bake – p.17	Honey Garlic Chicken with Quinoa – p.40	Baked Cinnamon Apples – p.48	Barley and Pomegranate Salad – p.65
30	Cheesy Mushroom and Herb Frittata – p.16	Beef and Sweet Potato Shepherd's Pie – p.42	Lemon Blueberry Greek Yogurt Cake – p.48	Lentil and Feta Salad – p.65

Notes: The 30-Day Meal Plan in this book is designed to guide and inspire your Crock Pot Diet journey. Caloric values are approximate and may vary based on portion sizes and specific ingredients. This plan offers a diverse, balanced menu rich in proteins, healthy fats, and carbohydrates, allowing you to maintain healthy eating without sacrificing deliciousness.

Feel free to adjust portion sizes to fit your personal dietary needs and goals. Whether you need to increase or decrease servings, tailor each meal to suit your preferences. Embrace creativity and enjoy each dish according to your individual requirements.

CHAPTER 3: BREAKFASTS:
Quick and Easy Egg Delights

Spinach and Feta Egg Casserole

Prep: 10 minutes | Cook: 4-6 hours | Serves: 4

Ingredients:

- 2 cups fresh spinach, chopped (60g)
- 1 cup crumbled feta cheese (150g)
- 8 large eggs
- 1/2 cup milk (120ml)
- 1 tsp salt (5g)
- 1/4 cup chopped green onions (30g)
- 1/2 tsp black pepper (2g)
- 1/2 tsp garlic powder (2g)
- 1/2 tsp low-carb sweetener (2g, optional)

Instructions:

1. Grease the Crock Pot with cooking spray.
2. In a large bowl, whisk eggs, milk, salt, pepper, garlic powder, and sweetener.
3. Stir in spinach, feta cheese, and green onions.
4. Pour the mixture into the Crock Pot.
5. Cover and cook on low for 4-6 hours until eggs are set.

Nutritional Facts (Per Serving): Calories: 600 | Sugars: 2g | Fat: 30g | Carbohydrates: 5g | Protein: 22g | Fiber: 6g | Sodium: 550mg

Cheesy Mushroom and Herb Frittata

Prep: 15 minutes | Cook: 4-6 hours | Serves: 4

Ingredients:

- 2 cups sliced mushrooms (200g)
- 1 cup shredded cheddar cheese (120g)
- 8 large eggs
- 1/2 cup milk (120ml)
- 1/4 cup chopped fresh herbs (parsley, chives) (30g)
- 1 tsp salt (5g)
- 1/2 tsp black pepper (2g)
- 1/2 tsp low-carb sweetener (2g)
- 1 tbsp olive oil (15ml)

Instructions:

1. Grease the Crock Pot with cooking spray.
2. Heat olive oil in a skillet over medium heat and sauté mushrooms until tender, about 5 minutes.
3. In a large bowl, whisk eggs, milk, salt, pepper, and sweetener.
4. Stir in sautéed mushrooms, cheddar cheese, and fresh herbs. Pour the mixture into the Crock Pot.
5. Cover and cook on low for 4-6 hours until eggs are set.

Nutritional Facts (Per Serving): Calories: 650 | Sugars: 3g | Fat: 32g | Carbohydrates: 5g | Protein: 25g | Fiber: 5g | Sodium: 600mg

Tomato Basil and Mozzarella Egg Bake

Prep: 10 minutes | Cook: 4-6 hours | Serves: 4

Ingredients:

- 2 cups cherry tomatoes, halved (300g)
- 1 cup shredded mozzarella cheese (120g)
- 8 large eggs
- 1/2 cup milk (120ml)
- 1/4 cup chopped fresh basil (30g)
- 1 tsp salt (5g)
- 1/2 tsp black pepper (2g)
- 1/2 tsp low-carb sweetener (2g)

Instructions:

1. Grease the Crock Pot with cooking spray.
2. In a large bowl, whisk eggs, milk, salt, pepper, and sweetener.
3. Stir in cherry tomatoes, mozzarella cheese, and basil.
4. Pour the mixture into the Crock Pot.
5. Cover and cook on low for 4-6 hours until eggs are set.

Nutritional Facts (Per Serving): Calories: 600 | Sugars: 4g | Fat: 30g | Carbohydrates: 4g | Protein: 23g | Fiber: 6g | Sodium: 570mg

Zucchini and Parmesan Egg Muffins

Prep: 10 minutes | Cook: 4-6 hours | Serves: 4

Ingredients:

- 2 cups shredded zucchini (240g)
- 1 cup grated Parmesan cheese (100g)
- 8 large eggs
- 1/2 cup Greek yogurt (120g)
- 1/4 cup chopped green onions (30g)
- 1 tsp salt (5g)
- 1/2 tsp black pepper (2g)
- 1/2 tsp low-carb sweetener (2g)

Instructions:

1. Grease the Crock Pot with cooking spray.
2. In a large bowl, whisk eggs, Greek yogurt, salt, pepper, and sweetener.
3. Stir in shredded zucchini, Parmesan cheese, and green onions.
4. Pour the mixture into silicone muffin cups and place them in the Crock Pot.
5. Cover and cook on low for 4-6 hours until eggs are set.

Nutritional Facts (Per Serving): Calories: 650 | Sugars: 3g | Fat: 25g | Carbohydrates: 3g | Protein: 25g | Fiber: 6g | Sodium: 550mg

Bacon and Mushroom Quiche

Prep: 15 minutes | Cook: 4-6 hours | Serves: 4

Ingredients:

- 1 cup cooked and crumbled bacon (150g)
- 2 cups sliced mushrooms (200g)
- 1 cup shredded cheddar cheese (120g)
- 8 large eggs
- 1/2 cup Greek yogurt (120g)
- 1/4 cup chopped fresh herbs (parsley, chives) (30g)
- 1 tsp salt (5g)
- 1/2 tsp black pepper (2g)
- 1/2 tsp low-carb sweetener (2g)
- 1 tbsp olive oil (15ml)

Instructions:

1. Grease the Crock Pot with cooking spray.
2. Heat olive oil in a skillet over medium heat and sauté mushrooms until tender, about 5 minutes.
3. In a large bowl, whisk eggs, Greek yogurt, salt, pepper, and sweetener.
4. Stir in sautéed mushrooms, cooked bacon, cheddar cheese, and fresh herbs.
5. Pour the mixture into the Crock Pot.
6. Cover and cook on low for 4-6 hours until eggs are set.

Nutritional Facts (Per Serving): Calories: 650 | Sugars: 4g | Fat: 28g | Carbohydrates: 3g | Protein: 24g | Fiber: 5g | Sodium: 600mg

Broccoli, Cheddar, and Salmon Breakfast Quiche

Prep: 15 minutes | Cook: 4-6 hours | Serves: 4

Ingredients:

- 2 cups chopped broccoli (180g)
- 1 cup shredded cheddar cheese (120g)
- 1 cup cooked, flaked salmon (200g)
- 8 large eggs
- 1/2 cup Greek yogurt (120g)
- 1/4 cup chopped green onions (30g)
- 1 tsp salt (5g)
- 1/2 tsp black pepper (2g)
- 1/2 tsp low-carb sweetener (2g)

Instructions:

1. Grease the Crock Pot with cooking spray.
2. In a large bowl, whisk eggs, Greek yogurt, salt, pepper, and sweetener.
3. Stir in chopped broccoli, cheddar cheese, flaked salmon, and green onions.
4. Pour the mixture into the Crock Pot.
5. Cover and cook on low for 4-6 hours until eggs are set.

Nutritional Facts (Per Serving): Calories: 650 | Sugars: 3g | Fat: 27g | Carbohydrates: 3g | Protein: 25g | Fiber: 6g | Sodium: 570mg

Ham and Cheese Breakfast Strata

Prep: 15 minutes | Cook: 6 hours | Serves: 4

Ingredients:

- 4 cups cubed whole grain bread (240g)
- 1 cup diced ham (150g)
- 1 cup shredded cheddar cheese (120g)
- 8 large eggs
- 1 cup milk (240ml)
- 1/2 cup Greek yogurt (120g)
- 1 tsp salt (5g)
- 1/2 tsp black pepper (2g)
- 1/2 tsp low-carb sweetener (2g)
- 1/4 cup chopped green onions (30g)

Instructions:

1. Grease the Crock Pot with cooking spray.
2. In a large bowl, whisk eggs, milk, Greek yogurt, salt, pepper, and sweetener.
3. Layer half of the bread cubes in the Crock Pot, followed by half of the ham and half of the cheese.
4. Repeat the layers with the remaining bread, ham, and cheese.
5. Pour the egg mixture evenly over the layers.
6. Sprinkle with chopped green onions.
7. Cover and cook on low for 6 hours until eggs are set.

Nutritional Facts (Per Serving): Calories: 600 | Sugars: 4g | Fat: 22g | Carbohydrates: 5g | Protein: 28g | Fiber: 5g | Sodium: 600mg

Southwestern Egg and Sausage Breakfast Bake

Prep: 15 minutes | Cook: 4-6 hours | Serves: 4

Ingredients:

- 1 lb ground sausage (450g)
- 1 cup diced bell peppers (150g)
- 1 cup shredded Mexican blend cheese (120g)
- 8 large eggs
- 1 cup milk (240ml)
- 1/2 cup Greek yogurt (120g)
- 1 tsp salt (5g)
- 1/2 tsp black pepper (2g)
- 1 tsp chili powder (5g)
- 1/4 cup chopped cilantro (30g)

Instructions:

1. Grease the Crock Pot with cooking spray.
2. In a skillet, cook sausage over medium heat until browned; drain excess fat.
3. In a large bowl, whisk eggs, milk, Greek yogurt, salt, pepper, and chili powder.
4. Stir in cooked sausage, bell peppers, and shredded cheese.
5. Pour the mixture into the Crock Pot.
6. Cover and cook on low for 4-6 hours until eggs are set.
7. Sprinkle with chopped cilantro before serving.

Nutritional Facts (Per Serving): Calories: 650 | Sugars: 5g | Fat: 25g | Carbohydrates: 3g | Protein: 26g | Fiber: 6g | Sodium: 600mg

CHAPTER 4: BREAKFASTS: Savory Whole Grain Porridges and Breakfast Bowls

Orange Zest Quinoa Breakfast Bowl

Prep: 10 minutes | Cook: 4-6 hours | Serves: 4

Ingredients:

- 1 cup quinoa (170g)
- 2 cups milk (480ml)
- 1/2 cup Greek yogurt (120g)
- 1 tbsp orange zest (6g)
- 2 medium oranges, segmented (300g)
- 1 tsp vanilla extract (5ml)
- 1/4 cup chopped nuts (almonds, walnuts) (30g)
- 1 tsp low-carb sweetener (5g)
- 1/4 tsp salt (1g)

Instructions:

1. Grease the Crock Pot with cooking spray.
2. In a large bowl, mix quinoa, milk, Greek yogurt, orange zest, vanilla extract, sweetener, and salt.
3. Pour the mixture into the Crock Pot.
4. Cover and cook on low for 4-6 hours until quinoa is tender.
5. Stir in orange segments and chopped nuts before serving.

Nutritional Facts (Per Serving): Calories: 600 | Sugars: 8g | Fat: 22g | Carbohydrates: 40g | Protein: 20g | Fiber: 7g | Sodium: 200mg

Couscous and Avocado Breakfast Bowl with Feta

Prep: 10 minutes | Cook: 4-6 hours | Serves: 4

Ingredients:

- 1 cup couscous (170g)
- 1 1/2 cups vegetable broth (360ml)
- 2 avocados, diced (400g)
- 1 cup crumbled feta cheese (150g)
- 1/4 cup chopped green onions (30g)
- 1 tbsp olive oil (15ml)
- 1 tsp salt (5g)
- 1/2 tsp black pepper (2g)
- 1/2 tsp low-carb sweetener (2g)

Instructions:

1. Grease the Crock Pot with cooking spray.
2. In a large bowl, combine couscous, vegetable broth, olive oil, salt, pepper, and sweetener.
3. Pour the mixture into the Crock Pot.
4. Cover and cook on low for 4-6 hours until couscous is tender.
5. Stir in diced avocado, feta cheese, and green onions before serving.

Nutritional Facts (Per Serving): Calories: 650 | Sugars: 4g | Fat: 25g | Carbohydrates: 36g | Protein: 22g | Fiber: 7g | Sodium: 600mg

Savory Oatmeal with Spinach and Poached Egg

Prep: 10 minutes | Cook: 4-6 hours | Serves: 4

Ingredients:

- 1 cup steel-cut oats (160g)
- 4 cups water (960ml)
- 2 cups fresh spinach, chopped (60g)
- 1/2 cup Greek yogurt (120g)
- 4 large eggs, poached
- 1 tsp salt (5g)
- 1/2 tsp black pepper (2g)
- 1/2 tsp low-carb sweetener (2g)

Instructions:

1. Grease the Crock Pot with cooking spray.
2. In a large bowl, combine steel-cut oats, water, salt, pepper, and sweetener.
3. Pour the mixture into the Crock Pot.
4. Cover and cook on low for 4-6 hours until oats are tender.
5. Stir in chopped spinach and Greek yogurt before serving.
6. Top each serving with a poached egg.

Nutritional Facts (Per Serving): Calories: 600 | Sugars: 3g | Fat: 20g | Carbohydrates: 38g | Protein: 23g | Fiber: 6g | Sodium: 500mg

Farro Breakfast Bowl with Roasted Vegetables

Prep: 15 minutes | Cook: 4-6 hours | Serves: 4

Ingredients:

- 1 cup farro (200g)
- 2 cups vegetable broth (480ml)
- 1 cup cherry tomatoes, halved (150g)
- 1 cup diced bell peppers (150g)
- 1 cup diced zucchini (150g)
- 1/2 cup Greek yogurt (120g)
- 1/4 cup chopped fresh herbs (parsley, thyme) (30g)
- 1 tbsp olive oil (15ml)
- 1 tsp salt (5g)
- 1/2 tsp black pepper (2g)
- 1/2 tsp low-carb sweetener (2g)

Instructions:

1. Grease the Crock Pot with cooking spray.
2. In a large bowl, combine farro, vegetable broth, olive oil, salt, pepper, and sweetener.
3. Add cherry tomatoes, bell peppers, and zucchini. Pour the mixture into the Crock Pot.
4. Cover and cook on low for 4-6 hours until farro is tender.
5. Stir in Greek yogurt and fresh herbs before serving.

Nutritional Facts (Per Serving): Calories: 600 | Sugars: 6g | Fat: 22g | Carbohydrates: 37g | Protein: 20g | Fiber: 7g | Sodium: 500mg

Green Buckwheat and Turkey Breakfast Bowl

Prep: 10 minutes | Cook: 4-6 hours | Serves: 4

Ingredients:

- 1 cup green buckwheat (180g)
- 2 cups water (480ml)
- 1 lb ground turkey (450g)
- 1 cup diced bell peppers (150g)
- 1/2 cup Greek yogurt (120g)
- 1/4 cup chopped parsley (30g)
- 1 tbsp olive oil (15ml)
- 1 tsp salt (5g)
- 1/2 tsp black pepper (2g)
- 1/2 tsp low-carb sweetener (2g)

Instructions:

1. Grease the Crock Pot with cooking spray.
2. Heat olive oil in a skillet over medium heat and cook ground turkey until browned.
3. In a large bowl, combine green buckwheat, water, cooked turkey, bell peppers, salt, pepper, and sweetener.
4. Pour the mixture into the Crock Pot.
5. Cover and cook on low for 4-6 hours until buckwheat is tender.
6. Stir in Greek yogurt and parsley before serving.

Nutritional Facts (Per Serving): Calories: 650 | Sugars: 3g | Fat: 22g | Carbohydrates: 36g | Protein: 26g | Fiber: 6g | Sodium: 500mg

Savory Amaranth with Bacon and Leeks

Prep: 15 minutes | Cook: 4-6 hours | Serves: 4

Ingredients:

- 1 cup amaranth (190g)
- 3 cups water (720ml)
- 1/2 lb bacon, chopped (225g)
- 1 cup sliced leeks (100g)
- 1/2 cup Greek yogurt (120g)
- 1/4 cup chopped chives (30g)
- 1 tbsp olive oil (15ml)
- 1 tsp salt (5g)
- 1/2 tsp black pepper (2g)
- 1/2 tsp low-carb sweetener (2g)

Instructions:

1. Grease the Crock Pot with cooking spray.
2. Cook bacon in a skillet until crispy; remove and set aside, leaving the fat in the skillet.
3. Sauté leeks in the bacon fat until tender.
4. In a large bowl, combine amaranth, water, cooked bacon, sautéed leeks, salt, pepper, and sweetener.
5. Pour the mixture into the Crock Pot.
6. Cover and cook on low for 4-6 hours until amaranth is tender.
7. Stir in Greek yogurt and chives before serving.

Nutritional Facts (Per Serving): Calories: 650 | Sugars: 4g | Fat: 24g | Carbohydrates: 35g | Protein: 24g | Fiber: 6g | Sodium: 600mg

Polenta with Roasted Tomatoes and Basil

Millet Porridge with Mushrooms and Herbs

Prep: 15 minutes | Cook: 4-6 hours | Serves: 4

Prep: 10 minutes | Cook: 4-6 hours | Serves: 4

Ingredients:

- 1 cup polenta (170g)
- 4 cups water (960ml)
- 1 cup cherry tomatoes, halved (150g)
- 1/2 cup shredded Parmesan cheese (50g)
- 1/4 cup chopped fresh basil (30g)
- 1 tbsp olive oil (15ml)
- 1 tsp salt (5g)
- 1/2 tsp black pepper (2g)
- 1/2 tsp low-carb sweetener (2g)

Ingredients:

- 1 cup millet (200g)
- 2 cups vegetable broth (480ml)
- 1 cup sliced mushrooms (100g)
- 1/4 cup chopped parsley (30g)
- 1 tbsp olive oil (15ml)
- 1 tsp salt (5g)
- 1/2 tsp black pepper (2g)
- 1/2 tsp low-carb sweetener (2g)
- 1 tsp dried thyme (5g)

Instructions:

1. Grease the Crock Pot with cooking spray.
2. In a large bowl, combine polenta, water, salt, pepper, and sweetener.
3. Pour the mixture into the Crock Pot and cover.
4. Cook on low for 4-6 hours until polenta is creamy.
5. In a skillet, heat olive oil over medium heat and roast cherry tomatoes until tender.
6. Stir roasted tomatoes and Parmesan cheese into the polenta.
7. Garnish with chopped basil before serving.

Nutritional Facts (Per Serving): Calories: 550 | Sugars: 5g | Fat: 21g | Carbohydrates: 40g | Protein: 20g | Fiber: 6g | Sodium: 500mg

Instructions:

1. Grease the Crock Pot with cooking spray.
2. In a large bowl, combine millet, vegetable broth, mushrooms, olive oil, salt, pepper, sweetener, and thyme.
3. Pour the mixture into the Crock Pot.
4. Cover and cook on low for 4-6 hours until millet is tender.
5. Stir in chopped parsley before serving.

Nutritional Facts (Per Serving): Calories: 650 | Sugars: 3g | Fat: 20g | Carbohydrates: 36g | Protein: 20g | Fiber: 6g | Sodium: 500mg

CHAPTER 5: BREAKFASTS: Protein-packed Ideas

Cottage Cheese and Raisin Berry Casserole

Prep: 15 minutes | Cook: 4-6 hours | Serves: 4

Ingredients:

- 2 cups cottage cheese (450g)
- 1 cup mixed berries (150g)
- 1/2 cup raisins (75g)
- 4 large eggs
- 1/2 cup Greek yogurt (120g)
- 1/4 cup low-carb sweetener (30g)
- 1 tsp vanilla extract (5ml)
- 1 tsp cinnamon (5g)
- 1/2 tsp salt (2g)

Instructions:

1. Grease the Crock Pot with cooking spray.
2. In a large bowl, whisk eggs, Greek yogurt, sweetener, vanilla extract, cinnamon, and salt.
3. Stir in cottage cheese, mixed berries, and raisins. Pour the mixture into the Crock Pot.
4. Cover and cook on low for 4-6 hours until set.

Nutritional Facts (Per Serving): Calories: 600 | Sugars: 8g | Fat: 20g | Carbohydrates: 38g | Protein: 28g | Fiber: 6g | Sodium: 400mg

Turkey Sausage, Zucchini, and Egg White Casserole

Prep: 15 minutes | Cook: 4-6 hours | Serves: 4

Ingredients:

- 1 lb turkey sausage, cooked and crumbled (450g)
- 2 cups diced zucchini (240g)
- 8 large egg whites
- 1/2 cup Greek yogurt (120g)
- 1 cup shredded mozzarella cheese (120g)
- 1/4 cup chopped green onions (30g)
- 1 tsp salt (5g)
- 1/2 tsp black pepper (2g)
- 1/2 tsp low-carb sweetener (2g)

Instructions:

1. Grease the Crock Pot with cooking spray.
2. In a large bowl, whisk egg whites, Greek yogurt, salt, pepper, and sweetener.
3. Stir in cooked turkey sausage, zucchini, mozzarella cheese, and green onions. Pour the mixture into the Crock Pot.
4. Cover and cook on low for 4-6 hours until eggs are set.

Nutritional Facts (Per Serving): Calories: 650 | Sugars: 3g | Fat: 22g | Carbohydrates: 34g | Protein: 30g | Fiber: 6g | Sodium: 600mg

Egg Muffins with Turkey and Spinach

Shrimp and Avocado Breakfast Frittata

Prep: 10 minutes | Cook: 4-6 hours | Serves: 4

Prep: 15 minutes | Cook: 4-6 hours | Serves: 4

Ingredients:

- 1 cup cooked, diced turkey (150g)
- 2 cups fresh spinach, chopped (60g)
- 8 large eggs
- 1/2 cup Greek yogurt (120g)
- 1/4 cup chopped green onions (30g)
- 1 tsp salt (5g)
- 1/2 tsp black pepper (2g)
- 1/2 tsp low-carb sweetener (2g)

Ingredients:

- 1 cup cooked shrimp, chopped (150g)
- 2 avocados, diced (400g)
- 8 large eggs
- 1/2 cup Greek yogurt (120g)
- 1 cup shredded mozzarella cheese (120g)
- 1/4 cup chopped cilantro (30g)
- 1 tsp salt (5g)
- 1/2 tsp black pepper (2g)
- 1/2 tsp low-carb sweetener (2g)

Instructions:

1. Grease the Crock Pot with cooking spray.
2. In a large bowl, whisk eggs, Greek yogurt, salt, pepper, and sweetener.
3. Stir in diced turkey, chopped spinach, and green onions.
4. Pour the mixture into silicone muffin cups and place them in the Crock Pot.
5. Cover and cook on low for 4-6 hours until eggs are set.

Instructions:

1. Grease the Crock Pot with cooking spray.
2. In a large bowl, whisk eggs, Greek yogurt, salt, pepper, and sweetener.
3. Stir in cooked shrimp, diced avocados, mozzarella cheese, and cilantro.
4. Pour the mixture into the Crock Pot.
Cover and cook on low for 4-6 hours until eggs are set.

Nutritional Facts (Per Serving): Calories: 600 | Sugars: 2g | Fat: 25g | Carbohydrates: 34g | Protein: 28g | Fiber: 6g | Sodium: 600mg

Nutritional Facts (Per Serving): Calories: 650 | Sugars: 3g | Fat: 26g | Carbohydrates: 35g | Protein: 25g | Fiber: 7g | Sodium: 500mg

Quinoa and Black Bean Breakfast Casserole

Prep: 15 minutes | Cook: 4-6 hours | Serves: 4

Ingredients:

- 1 cup quinoa, rinsed (170g)
- 2 cups vegetable broth (480ml)
- 1 cup canned black beans, rinsed and drained (170g)
- 1 cup diced bell peppers (150g)
- 1 cup diced tomatoes (150g)
- 8 large eggs
- 1/2 cup Greek yogurt (120g)
- 1 cup shredded cheddar cheese (120g)
- 1 tsp salt (5g)
- 1/2 tsp black pepper (2g)
- 1/2 tsp low-carb sweetener (2g)
- 1/4 cup chopped green onions (30g)

Instructions:

1. Grease the Crock Pot with cooking spray.
2. In a large bowl, whisk eggs, Greek yogurt, salt, pepper, and sweetener.
3. Stir in rinsed quinoa, vegetable broth, black beans, bell peppers, tomatoes, and shredded cheddar cheese.
4. Pour the mixture into the Crock Pot.
5. Cover and cook on low for 4-6 hours until eggs are set.
6. Sprinkle with chopped green onions before serving.

Nutritional Facts (Per Serving): Calories: 650 | Sugars: 5g | Fat: 20g | Carbohydrates: 36g | Protein: 27g | Fiber: 7g | Sodium: 550mg

Savory Lentil and Sausage Breakfast Stew

Prep: 15 minutes | Cook: 6 hours | Serves: 4

Ingredients:

- 1 cup lentils (200g)
- 4 cups chicken broth (960ml)
- 1 lb sausage, sliced (450g)
- 1 cup diced carrots (130g)
- 1 cup diced celery (100g)
- 1 cup diced onion (150g)
- 2 cloves garlic, minced (6g)
- 1 tsp salt (5g)
- 1/2 tsp black pepper (2g)
- 1 tsp dried thyme (5g)
- 1/2 tsp low-carb sweetener (2g)

Instructions:

1. Grease the Crock Pot with cooking spray.
2. In a large bowl, combine lentils, chicken broth, sausage, carrots, celery, onion, garlic, salt, pepper, thyme, and sweetener.
3. Pour the mixture into the Crock Pot.
4. Cover and cook on low for 6 hours until lentils are tender.

Nutritional Facts (Per Serving): Calories: 650 | Sugars: 3g | Fat: 20g | Carbohydrates: 38g | Protein: 30g | Fiber: 7g | Sodium: 600mg

Protein-Packed Veggie Omelette

Prep: 10 minutes | Cook: 4-6 hours | Serves: 4

Ingredients:

- 8 large eggs
- 1 cup egg whites (240ml)
- 1 cup diced bell peppers (150g)
- 1 cup chopped spinach (60g)
- 1/2 cup diced tomatoes (75g)
- 1/4 cup chopped onions (30g)
- 1/2 cup shredded cheddar cheese (60g)
- 1/2 cup Greek yogurt (120g)
- 1 tsp salt (5g)
- 1/2 tsp black pepper (2g)
- 1/2 tsp low-carb sweetener (2g)

Instructions:

1. Grease the Crock Pot with cooking spray.
2. In a large bowl, whisk eggs, egg whites, Greek yogurt, salt, pepper, and sweetener.
3. Stir in bell peppers, spinach, tomatoes, onions, and shredded cheddar cheese.
4. Pour the mixture into the Crock Pot.
5. Cover and cook on low for 4-6 hours until eggs are set.

Nutritional Facts (Per Serving): Calories: 650 | Sugars: 4g | Fat: 25g | Carbohydrates: 30g | Protein: 31g | Fiber: 6g | Sodium: 550mg

Spinach and Feta Stuffed Peppers

Prep: 15 minutes | Cook: 4-6 hours | Serves: 4

Ingredients:

- 4 large bell peppers, tops removed and seeds discarded
- 2 cups chopped spinach (120g)
- 1 cup crumbled feta cheese (150g)
- 8 large egg whites
- 1/2 cup Greek yogurt (120g)
- 1/4 cup chopped green onions (30g)
- 1 tsp salt (5g)
- 1/2 tsp black pepper (2g)
- 1/2 tsp low-carb sweetener (2g)

Instructions:

1. Grease the Crock Pot with cooking spray.
2. In a large bowl, whisk egg whites, Greek yogurt, salt, pepper, and sweetener.
3. Stir in chopped spinach, feta cheese, and green onions.
4. Stuff the bell peppers with the mixture and place them in the Crock Pot.
5. Cover and cook on low for 4-6 hours until peppers are tender and filling is set.

Nutritional Facts (Per Serving): Calories: 650 | Sugars: 5g | Fat: 22g | Carbohydrates: 32g | Protein: 28g | Fiber: 7g | Sodium: 600mg

CHAPTER 6: BREAKFASTS: Healthy Family Brunch Options

Quiche Lorraine

Prep: 15 minutes | Cook: 4-6 hours | Serves: 4

Ingredients:

- 1 pre-made pie crust (200g)
- 8 slices bacon, cooked and crumbled (200g)
- 1 cup shredded Swiss cheese (120g)
- 4 large eggs
- 1 cup heavy cream (240ml)
- 1/2 cup Greek yogurt (120g)
- 1/4 cup chopped green onions (30g)
- 1 tsp salt (5g)
- 1/2 tsp black pepper (2g)
- 1/2 tsp low-carb sweetener (2g)

Instructions:

1. Grease the Crock Pot with cooking spray.
2. Fit the pie crust into the bottom of the Crock Pot.
3. In a large bowl, whisk eggs, heavy cream, Greek yogurt, salt, pepper, and sweetener.
4. Stir in cooked bacon, Swiss cheese, and green onions. Pour the mixture into the pie crust.
5. Cover and cook on low for 4-6 hours until quiche is set.

Nutritional Facts (Per Serving): Calories: 650 | Sugars: 3g | Fat: 25g | Carbohydrates: 34g | Protein: 25g | Fiber: 5g | Sodium: 600mg

Eggplant Parmesan

Prep: 20 minutes | Cook: 4-6 hours | Serves: 4

Ingredients:

- 2 large eggplants, sliced (500g)
- 2 cups marinara sauce (480ml)
- 2 cups shredded mozzarella cheese (240g)
- 1 cup grated Parmesan cheese (100g)
- 1/2 cup breadcrumbs (60g)
- 1/4 cup chopped fresh basil (30g)
- 2 large eggs, beaten
- 1/2 cup flour (60g)
- 1 tsp salt (5g)
- 1/2 tsp black pepper (2g)
- 1 tbsp olive oil (15ml)

Instructions:

1. Grease the Crock Pot with cooking spray.
2. Bread eggplant slices: coat with flour, dip in beaten eggs, then breadcrumbs.
3. Brown slices in olive oil on medium heat.
4. Layer marinara sauce at the bottom of the Crock Pot.
5. Add layers of eggplant, mozzarella, Parmesan, and basil. Repeat until all ingredients are used.
6. Cover and cook on low for 4–6 hours until eggplant is tender.

Nutritional Facts (Per Serving): Calories: 650 | Sugars: 7g | Fat: 22g | Carbohydrates: 40g | Protein: 25g | Fiber: 6g | Sodium: 600mg

Pepperoni and Cheese Crock Pot Pizza

Prep: 15 minutes | Cook: 4-6 hours | Serves: 4

Ingredients:

- 1 pre-made pizza dough (250g)
- 1 cup pizza sauce (240ml)
- 2 cups shredded mozzarella cheese (240g)
- 1/2 cup sliced pepperoni (60g)
- 1/4 cup grated Parmesan cheese (25g)
- 1 tsp Italian seasoning (5g)
- 1/2 tsp garlic powder (2g)
- 1/2 tsp low-carb sweetener (2g)

Instructions:

1. Grease the Crock Pot with cooking spray.
2. Roll out the pizza dough and fit it into the bottom of the Crock Pot.
3. Spread pizza sauce over the dough.
4. Sprinkle mozzarella cheese evenly over the sauce.
5. Arrange pepperoni slices on top of the cheese.
6. Sprinkle with Parmesan cheese, Italian seasoning, garlic powder, and sweetener.
7. Cover and cook on high for 4-6 hours until crust is cooked and cheese is melted.
8. For a crispy crust, finish under a broiler for a few minutes before serving.

Nutritional Facts (Per Serving): Calories: 650 | Sugars: 5g | Fat: 24g | Carbohydrates: 38g | Protein: 26g | Fiber: 5g | Sodium: 600mg

Margherita Crock Pot Pizza

Prep: 15 minutes | Cook: 2 hours | Serves: 4

Ingredients:

- 1 pre-made pizza dough (250g)
- 1 cup tomato sauce (240ml)
- 8 oz fresh mozzarella, sliced (225g)
- 1/4 cup fresh basil leaves (10g)
- 1 tbsp olive oil (15ml)
- 1/2 tsp salt (2g)
- 1/2 tsp black pepper (2g)
- 1/2 tsp low-carb sweetener (2g)

Instructions:

1. Grease the Crock Pot with cooking spray.
2. Roll out the pizza dough and fit it into the bottom of the Crock Pot.
3. Spread tomato sauce over the dough.
4. Arrange fresh mozzarella slices on top of the sauce.
5. Sprinkle with salt, pepper, and sweetener.
6. Drizzle with olive oil.
7. Cover and cook on high for 4-6 hours until crust is cooked and cheese is melted.
8. Top with fresh basil leaves before serving.

Nutritional Facts (Per Serving): Calories: 650 | Sugars: 3g | Fat: 22g | Carbohydrates: 38g | Protein: 22g | Fiber: 5g | Sodium: 600mg

Grilled Vegetable and Hummus Wrap

Prep: 15 minutes | Cook: 4-6 hours | Serves: 4

Ingredients:

- 2 cups sliced bell peppers (300g)
- 1 cup sliced zucchini (150g)
- 1 cup sliced eggplant (150g)
- 1/4 cup olive oil (60ml)
- 1 tsp salt (5g)
- 1/2 tsp black pepper (2g)
- 1 tsp dried oregano (5g)
- 4 large whole wheat tortillas (240g)
- 1 cup hummus (240g)
- 1/4 cup chopped fresh parsley (15g)

Instructions:

1. Grease the Crock Pot with cooking spray.
2. In a large bowl, toss bell peppers, zucchini, and eggplant with olive oil, salt, pepper, and oregano.
3. Pour the vegetable mixture into the Crock Pot.
4. Cover and cook on low for 4-6 hours until vegetables are tender.
5. Spread hummus on each tortilla, top with grilled vegetables and fresh parsley.
6. Roll up the tortillas and serve.

Nutritional Facts (Per Serving): Calories: 650 | Sugars: 4g | Fat: 24g | Carbohydrates: 40g | Protein: 16g | Fiber: 7g | Sodium: 600mg

Lemon Blueberry French Toast Casserole

Prep: 15 minutes | Cook: 6 hours | Serves: 4

Ingredients:

- 8 cups cubed French bread (400g)
- 2 cups fresh blueberries (300g)
- 6 large eggs
- 1 cup milk (240ml)
- 1/2 cup Greek yogurt (120g)
- 1/4 cup lemon juice (60ml)
- 1 tbsp lemon zest (6g)
- 1/2 cup low-carb sweetener (60g)
- 1 tsp vanilla extract (5ml)
- 1/2 tsp salt (2g)

Instructions:

1. Grease the Crock Pot with cooking spray.
2. In a large bowl, whisk eggs, milk, Greek yogurt, lemon juice, lemon zest, sweetener, vanilla extract, and salt.
4. Stir in cubed French bread and blueberries.
5. Pour the mixture into the Crock Pot.
6. Cover and cook on low for 6 hours until set and golden.
7. Serve warm.

Nutritional Facts (Per Serving): Calories: 600 | Sugars: 7g | Fat: 18g | Carbohydrates: 40g | Protein: 20g | Fiber: 6g | Sodium: 500mg

CHAPTER 7: LUNCHES: Hearty Soups and Stews

Beef and Barley Stew

Prep: 20 minutes | Cook: 8 hours | Serves: 6

Ingredients:

- 1.5 lbs beef stew meat, cubed (680g)
- 1 large onion, chopped (150g)
- 3 cloves garlic, minced
- 4 cups beef broth (1 liter)
- 1 cup pearl barley (200g)
- 2 cups diced carrots (300g)
- 2 cups diced celery (300g)
- 1 can diced tomatoes (28 oz/800g)
- 1 tsp dried thyme
- 1 tsp dried rosemary
- Salt and pepper to taste
- 2 tbsp chopped parsley

Instructions:

1. Grease the Crock Pot with cooking spray.
2. Add beef, onion, garlic, beef broth, barley, carrots, celery, tomatoes, thyme, rosemary, salt, and pepper to the Crock Pot.
3. Cover and cook on low for 8 hours until beef is tender and barley is cooked.
4. Stir in parsley before serving.

Nutritional Facts (Per Serving): Calories: 650 | Sugars: 5g | Fat: 20g | Carbohydrates: 35g | Protein: 30g | Fiber: 8g | Sodium: 600mg

Beef and Sweet Potato Ragout

Prep: 20 minutes | Cook: 8 hours | Serves: 6

Ingredients:

- 1.5 lbs beef stew meat, cubed (680g)
- 1 large onion, chopped (150g)
- 3 cloves garlic, minced
- 4 cups beef broth (1 liter)
- 3 cups diced sweet potatoes (450g)
- 2 cups diced carrots (300g)
- 1 can diced tomatoes (28 oz/800g)
- 1 tsp ground cumin
- 1 tsp paprika
- 1 tsp dried thyme
- Salt and pepper to taste
- 2 tbsp chopped cilantro

Instructions:

1. Grease the Crock Pot with cooking spray.
2. Add beef, onion, garlic, beef broth, sweet potatoes, carrots, tomatoes, cumin, paprika, thyme, salt, and pepper to the Crock Pot.
3. Cover and cook on low for 8 hours until beef and sweet potatoes are tender.
4. Stir in cilantro before serving.

Nutritional Facts (Per Serving): Calories: 600 | Sugars: 6g | Fat: 20g | Carbohydrates: 40g | Protein: 30g | Fiber: 8g | Sodium: 700mg

Chicken Noodle Soup

Prep: 20 minutes | Cook: 6 hours | Serves: 6

Ingredients:

- 1 lb boneless, skinless chicken breasts (450g)
- 8 cups chicken broth (2 liters)
- 2 cups sliced carrots (300g)
- 2 cups sliced celery (300g)
- 1 large onion, chopped (150g)
- 3 cloves garlic, minced
- 1 tsp dried thyme
- 1 tsp dried rosemary
- 2 bay leaves
- Salt and pepper to taste
- 2 cups egg noodles (200g)
- 2 tbsp chopped parsley

Instructions:

1. Place chicken breasts, chicken broth, carrots, celery, onion, garlic, thyme, rosemary, bay leaves, salt, and pepper in the Crock Pot.
2. Cover and cook on low for 6 hours.
3. Remove chicken, shred with two forks, and return to the pot.
4. Add egg noodles and cook on high for another 20 minutes until noodles are tender.
5. Remove bay leaves and sprinkle with chopped parsley before serving.

Nutritional Facts (Per Serving): Calories: 600 | Sugars: 6g | Fat: 15g | Carbohydrates: 38g | Protein: 35g | Fiber: 8g | Sodium: 700mg

Creamy Mushroom and Wild Rice Soup

Prep: 15 minutes | Cook: 6 hours | Serves: 6

Ingredients:

- 1 cup wild rice, uncooked (200g)
- 8 cups vegetable broth (2 liters)
- 1 lb mushrooms, sliced (450g)
- 1 large onion, chopped (150g)
- 3 cloves garlic, minced
- 2 cups chopped carrots (300g)
- 2 cups chopped celery (300g)
- 1 tsp dried thyme
- 1 tsp dried rosemary
- 1 cup heavy cream (240ml)
- Salt and pepper to taste
- 2 tbsp chopped parsley

Instructions:

1. Add wild rice, vegetable broth, mushrooms, onion, garlic, carrots, celery, thyme, and rosemary to the Crock Pot.
2. Cover and cook on low for 6 hours.
3. Stir in heavy cream, salt, and pepper. Cook on high for another 10 minutes.
Garnish with chopped parsley before serving.

Nutritional Facts (Per Serving): Calories: 650 | Sugars: 5g | Fat: 25g | Carbohydrates: 38g | Protein: 25g | Fiber: 9g | Sodium: 600mg

Creamy Broccoli and Cheddar Soup

Prep: 15 minutes | Cook: 4 hours | Serves: 6

Ingredients:

- 4 cups broccoli florets (600g)
- 8 cups chicken broth (2 liters)
- 1 large onion, chopped (150g)
- 3 cloves garlic, minced
- 2 cups chopped carrots (300g)
- 2 cups chopped celery (300g)
- 1 cup heavy cream (240ml)
- 2 cups shredded cheddar cheese (200g)
- 1 tsp dried thyme
- Salt and pepper to taste

Instructions:

1. Add broccoli, chicken broth, onion, garlic, carrots, celery, and thyme to the Crock Pot.
2. Cover and cook on low for 6 hours.
3. Use an immersion blender to puree the soup until smooth.
4. Stir in heavy cream and cheddar cheese until melted and smooth.
5. Season with salt and pepper to taste before serving.

Nutritional Facts (Per Serving): Calories: 650 | Sugars: 5g | Fat: 30g | Carbohydrates: 30g | Protein: 25g | Fiber: 7g | Sodium: 700mg

Vegetable Minestrone

Prep: 15 minutes | Cook: 6 hours | Serves: 6

Ingredients:

- 1 large onion, chopped (150g)
- 3 cloves garlic, minced
- 2 cups diced carrots (300g)
- 2 cups diced celery (300g)
- 2 cups diced zucchini (300g)
- 1 can diced tomatoes (28 oz/800g)
- 4 cups vegetable broth (1 liter)
- 1 can kidney beans, drained and rinsed (15 oz/425g)
- 1 cup small pasta (150g)
- 1 tsp dried oregano
- 1 tsp dried basil
- 1 tsp dried thyme
- Salt and pepper to taste
- 2 cups chopped spinach (60g)

Instructions:

1. Add onion, garlic, carrots, celery, zucchini, tomatoes, vegetable broth, kidney beans, oregano, basil, thyme, salt, and pepper to the Crock Pot.
2. Cover and cook on low for 6 hours.
3. Add pasta and spinach in the last 30 minutes of cooking on high.

Nutritional Facts (Per Serving): Calories: 600 | Sugars: 6g | Fat: 20g | Carbohydrates: 40g | Protein: 30g | Fiber: 8g | Sodium: 700mg

Butternut Squash and Red Lentil Stew

Prep: 15 minutes | Cook: 6 hours | Serves: 6

Ingredients:

- 1 large onion, chopped (150g)
- 3 cloves garlic, minced
- 4 cups butternut squash, peeled and diced (600g)
- 2 cups red lentils (400g)
- 8 cups vegetable broth (2 liters)
- 1 can diced tomatoes (28 oz/800g)
- 2 cups chopped carrots (300g)
- 1 tsp ground cumin
- 1 tsp ground coriander
- 1 tsp turmeric
- Salt and pepper to taste
- 2 tbsp chopped cilantro

Instructions:

1. Grease the Crock Pot with cooking spray.
2. Add onion, garlic, butternut squash, red lentils, vegetable broth, diced tomatoes, carrots, cumin, coriander, turmeric, salt, and pepper to the Crock Pot.
3. Cover and cook on low for 6 hours until lentils and squash are tender.
4. Garnish with chopped cilantro before serving.

Nutritional Facts (Per Serving): Calories: 600 | Sugars: 5g | Fat: 20g | Carbohydrates: 35g | Protein: 30g | Fiber: 8g | Sodium: 700mg

Turkey and Quinoa Chili

Prep: 15 minutes | Cook: 6 hours | Serves: 6

Ingredients:

- 1 lb ground turkey (450g)
- 1 large onion, chopped (150g)
- 3 cloves garlic, minced
- 1 can diced tomatoes (28 oz/800g)
- 2 cups chicken broth (500ml)
- 1 cup quinoa, rinsed (200g)
- 1 can black beans, drained and rinsed (15 oz/425g)
- 1 can kidney beans, drained and rinsed (15 oz/425g)
- 1 cup corn kernels (150g)
- 2 tbsp chili powder
- 1 tsp ground cumin
- 1 tsp smoked paprika
- Salt and pepper to taste
- 2 tbsp chopped cilantro

Instructions:

1. Grease the Crock Pot with cooking spray.
2. Brown the ground turkey in a skillet over medium heat, then transfer to the Crock Pot.
3. Add onion, garlic, diced tomatoes, chicken broth, quinoa, black beans, kidney beans, corn, chili powder, cumin, smoked paprika, salt, and pepper to the Crock Pot.
4. Cover and cook on low for 6 hours until quinoa and beans are tender.
5. Garnish with chopped cilantro before serving.

Nutritional Facts (Per Serving): Calories: 600 | Sugars: 5g | Fat: 20g | Carbohydrates: 35g | Protein: 30g | Fiber: 8g | Sodium: 700mg

Chicken and Vegetable Ragout

Prep: 20 minutes | Cook: 6 hours | Serves: 6

Ingredients:

- 1.5 lbs boneless, skinless chicken thighs, cubed (680g)
- 1 large onion, chopped (150g)
- 3 cloves garlic, minced
- 4 cups chicken broth (1 liter)
- 2 cups diced carrots (300g)
- 2 cups diced parsnips (300g)
- 2 cups diced potatoes (300g)
- 1 cup green beans, chopped (150g)
- 1 tsp dried thyme
- 1 tsp dried rosemary
- Salt and pepper to taste
- 2 tbsp chopped parsley

Instructions:

1. Grease the Crock Pot with cooking spray.
2. Add chicken, onion, garlic, chicken broth, carrots, parsnips, potatoes, green beans, thyme, rosemary, salt, and pepper to the Crock Pot.
3. Cover and cook on low for 6 hours until vegetables are tender.
4. Stir in parsley before serving.

Nutritional Facts (Per Serving): Calories: 650 | Sugars: 5g | Fat: 25g | Carbohydrates: 35g | Protein: 30g | Fiber: 8g | Sodium: 700mg

Mediterranean Vegetable Ragout

Prep: 15 minutes | Cook: 6 hours | Serves: 6

Ingredients:

- 1 large eggplant, diced (300g)
- 2 zucchinis, diced (300g)
- 1 large onion, chopped (150g)
- 3 cloves garlic, minced
- 1 can diced tomatoes (28 oz/800g)
- 1 cup vegetable broth (250ml)
- 1 red bell pepper, chopped (150g)
- 1 yellow bell pepper, chopped (150g)
- 2 tbsp olive oil
- 1 tsp dried oregano
- 1 tsp dried basil
- Salt and pepper to taste
- 2 tbsp chopped fresh parsley

Instructions:

1. Grease the Crock Pot with cooking spray.
2. Add eggplant, zucchinis, onion, garlic, tomatoes, vegetable broth, red and yellow bell peppers, olive oil, oregano, basil, salt, and pepper to the Crock Pot.
3. Cover and cook on low for 6 hours until vegetables are tender.
4. Stir in fresh parsley before serving.

Nutritional Facts (Per Serving): Calories: 650 | Sugars: 6g | Fat: 25g | Carbohydrates: 35g | Protein: 30g | Fiber: 8g | Sodium: 700mg

CHAPTER 8: LUNCHES:
Nutritious Grain and Legume Dishes

Farro and Apple Salad

Prep: 15 minutes | Cook: 1 hour | Serves: 6

Ingredients:

- 2 cups cooked farro (300g)
- 2 large apples, diced (300g)
- 1 cup chopped walnuts (100g)
- 1 cup diced celery (150g)
- 1/4 cup olive oil (60ml)
- 2 tbsp apple cider vinegar
- 1 tbsp honey
- Salt and pepper to taste
- 2 tbsp chopped fresh parsley
- 1/2 cup dried cranberries (75g)

Instructions:

1. Add uncooked farro and 4 cups water or broth to the Crock Pot. Cook on low for 1 hour until tender, adding more liquid if needed.
2. In a large bowl, mix cooked farro, apples, walnuts, celery, and dried cranberries.
3. Whisk together olive oil, apple cider vinegar, honey, salt, and pepper in a small bowl.
4. Pour dressing over the salad, toss to combine, and garnish with fresh parsley before serving.

Nutritional Facts (Per Serving): Calories: 600 | Sugars: 8g | Fat: 25g | Carbohydrates: 40g | Protein: 25g | Fiber: 9g | Sodium: 200mg

Quinoa and Black Bean Salad

Prep: 15 minutes | Cook: 45 minutes | Serves: 6

Ingredients:

- 2 cups cooked quinoa (300g)
- 1 can black beans, drained and rinsed (15 oz/425g)
- 1 cup corn kernels (150g)
- 1 avocado, diced (150g)
- 1 red bell pepper, diced (150g)
- 1/4 cup chopped red onion (40g)
- 1/4 cup chopped cilantro (15g)
- 1/4 cup olive oil (60ml)
- 2 tbsp lime juice
- 1 tsp ground cumin
- Salt and pepper to taste

Instructions:

1. Add rinsed quinoa and 2 cups broth to the Crock Pot. Cook on low for 45 minutes. Fluff and cool.
2. Mix Ingredients: In a bowl, combine cooked quinoa, black beans, corn, avocado, bell pepper, red onion, and cilantro.
3. Add Dressing: Whisk olive oil, lime juice, cumin, salt, and pepper. Pour over salad and toss.

Nutritional Facts (Per Serving): Calories: 600 | Sugars: 5g | Fat: 25g | Carbohydrates: 40g | Protein: 25g | Fiber: 8g | Sodium: 400mg

Wild Rice and Cranberry Salad

Prep: 15 minutes | Cook: 1 hour | Serves: 6

Ingredients:

- 2 cups cooked wild rice (300g)
- 1 cup dried cranberries (150g)
- 1 cup toasted almonds, sliced (100g)
- 1 large apple, diced (150g)
- 1/4 cup chopped red onion (40g)
- 1/4 cup olive oil (60ml)
- 2 tbsp apple cider vinegar
- 1 tbsp honey
- Salt and pepper to taste
- 2 tbsp chopped fresh parsley

Instructions:

1. Add uncooked wild rice and 4 cups water or vegetable broth to the Crock Pot.
2. Cover and cook on low for 1 hour or until wild rice is tender. If necessary, add more liquid to prevent drying out.
3. In a large bowl, combine cooked wild rice, dried cranberries, toasted almonds, apple, and red onion.
4. In a small bowl, whisk together olive oil, apple cider vinegar, honey, salt, and pepper.
5. Pour dressing over salad and toss to combine.
6. Garnish with fresh parsley before serving.

Nutritional Facts (Per Serving): Calories: 600 | Sugars: 8g | Fat: 25g | Carbohydrates: 40g | Protein: 25g | Fiber: 9g | Sodium: 200mg

Lentil and Vegetable

Prep: 15 minutes | Cook: 45 minutes | Serves: 6

Ingredients:

- 2 cups cooked lentils (300g)
- 1 cup chopped bell peppers (150g)
- 1 cup chopped carrots (150g)
- 1 cup chopped broccoli (150g)
- 1 cup chopped zucchini (150g)
- 1 large onion, chopped (150g)
- 3 cloves garlic, minced
- 1/4 cup soy sauce (60ml)
- 2 tbsp olive oil
- 1 tsp ground cumin
- 1 tsp ground coriander
- Salt and pepper to taste
- 2 tbsp chopped fresh cilantro

Instructions:

1. Add rinsed lentils and 3 cups vegetable broth to the Crock Pot. Cook on low for 45 minutes until tender. Drain excess liquid if needed.
2. In a large bowl, mix cooked lentils with bell peppers, carrots, broccoli, zucchini, onion, and garlic.
3. Whisk together soy sauce, olive oil, cumin, coriander, salt, and pepper in a small bowl.
4. Pour the dressing over the mixture, toss to combine, and garnish with fresh cilantro.

Nutritional Facts (Per Serving): Calories: 600 | Sugars: 5g | Fat: 20g | Carbohydrates: 40g | Protein: 30g | Fiber: 8g | Sodium: 700mg

CHAPTER 9: LUNCHES:
Gourmet Pasta and Risotto

Spinach and Ricotta Stuffed Shells

Prep: 20 minutes | Cook: 4 hours | Serves: 6

Ingredients:

- 12 oz jumbo pasta shells (340g)
- 2 cups ricotta cheese (450g)
- 1 cup shredded mozzarella cheese (100g)
- 1 cup grated Parmesan cheese (100g)
- 2 cups fresh spinach, chopped (60g)
- 1 large egg, beaten
- 1 tsp dried oregano
- 1 tsp dried basil
- 4 cups marinara sauce (1 liter)
- Salt and pepper to taste

Instructions:

1. Cook pasta shells according to package directions; drain and set aside.
2. In a bowl, combine ricotta, mozzarella, Parmesan, spinach, egg, oregano, basil, salt, and pepper. Stuff each shell with the cheese mixture.
3. Pour 2 cups of marinara sauce in the bottom of the Crock Pot.
4. Arrange stuffed shells over the sauce, top with remaining sauce and cook on low for 4 hours.

Nutritional Facts (Per Serving): Calories: 600 | Sugars: 6g | Fat: 25g | Carbohydrates: 35g | Protein: 30g | Fiber: 8g | Sodium: 700mg

Gorgonzola and Pear Risotto

Prep: 15 minutes | Cook: 3 hours | Serves: 6

Ingredients:

- 2 cups Arborio rice (400g)
- 4 cups chicken broth (1 liter)
- 2 ripe pears, diced (300g)
- 1 large onion, chopped (150g)
- 3 cloves garlic, minced
- 1 cup dry white wine (240ml)
- 1 cup crumbled Gorgonzola cheese (150g)
- 1/4 cup heavy cream (60ml)
- 2 tbsp olive oil
- 1 tbsp fresh thyme, chopped
- Salt and pepper to taste

Instructions:

1. Heat olive oil in a skillet and sauté onion and garlic until soft.
2. Add Arborio rice and cook for 2 minutes, then add wine and cook until absorbed.
3. Transfer mixture to the Crock Pot and add chicken broth and pears.
4. Cover and cook on high for 3 hours.
5. Stir in Gorgonzola, cream, thyme, salt, and pepper before serving.

Nutritional Facts (Per Serving): Calories: 600 | Sugars: 6g | Fat: 25g | Carbohydrates: 40g | Protein: 25g | Fiber: 8g | Sodium: 700mg

Creamy Tomato and Basil Pasta

Prep: 15 minutes | Cook: 4 hours | Serves: 6

Ingredients:

- 1 lb (450g) sturdy pasta (such as penne, rigatoni, or fusilli)
- 2 cups tomato sauce (500ml)
- 1 cup heavy cream (240ml)
- 1 large onion, chopped (150g)
- 1/4 cup chopped fresh basil (15g)
- 1/4 cup grated Parmesan cheese (30g)
- 2 tbsp olive oil
- 1 tsp dried oregano
- Salt and pepper to taste
- 3 cloves garlic, minced

Instructions:

1. Add pasta, tomato sauce, heavy cream, chopped onion, minced garlic, grated Parmesan, olive oil, dried oregano, salt, and pepper to the Crock Pot.
2. Cover and cook on low for 2 hours.
3. Stir the pasta to prevent sticking. If the mixture is too thick, add an additional 1/2 cup (120ml) of water, chicken broth, or more heavy cream.
4. Cover and cook on low for another 2 hours until pasta is tender and creamy.
5. Stir in chopped fresh basil.

Nutritional Facts (Per Serving): Calories: 600 | Sugars: 6g | Fat: 25g | Carbohydrates: 40g | Protein: 25g | Fiber: 7g | Sodium: 600mg

Butternut Squash and Sage Risotto

Prep: 15 minutes | Cook: 3 hours | Serves: 6

Ingredients:

- 2 cups Arborio rice (400g)
- 4 cups vegetable broth (1 liter)
- 2 cups butternut squash, diced (300g)
- 1 large onion, chopped (150g)
- 3 cloves garlic, minced
- 1 cup dry white wine (240ml)
- 1/2 cup grated Parmesan cheese (50g)
- 1/4 cup heavy cream (60ml)
- 2 tbsp olive oil
- 1 tbsp fresh sage, chopped
- Salt and pepper to taste

Instructions:

1. Heat olive oil in a skillet and sauté onion and garlic until soft.
2. Add Arborio rice and cook for 2 minutes, then add wine and cook until absorbed.
3. Transfer mixture to the Crock Pot and add vegetable broth and butternut squash.
4. Cover and cook on high for 3 hours. Check the consistency of the rice before adding the cream and cheese, and add more broth if necessary.
5. Stir in Parmesan, cream, sage, salt, and pepper before serving.

Nutritional Facts (Per Serving): Calories: 600 | Sugars: 5g | Fat: 25g | Carbohydrates: 40g | Protein: 25g | Fiber: 8g | Sodium: 700mg

Beef Stroganoff with Whole-Grain Noodles

Prep: 20 minutes | Cook: 8 hours | Serves: 6

Ingredients:

- 1.5 lbs beef stew meat, cubed (680g)
- 1 large onion, chopped (150g)
- 3 cloves garlic, minced
- 8 oz mushrooms, sliced (225g)
- 2 cups beef broth (500ml)
- 1 cup sour cream (240ml)
- 2 tbsp flour (30g)
- 1 tbsp Dijon mustard
- 1 tsp dried thyme
- Salt and pepper to taste
- 12 oz whole-grain noodles (340g)
- 2 tbsp chopped fresh parsley

Instructions:

1. Add beef, onion, garlic, mushrooms, beef broth, Dijon mustard, thyme, salt, and pepper to the Crock Pot.
2. Cover and cook on low for 8 hours.
3. Mix sour cream and flour, then stir into the Crock Pot. Cook for an additional 30 minutes.
4. Add the whole-grain noodles 1 hour before the end of cooking on high temperature.
5. Serve beef stroganoff over noodles and garnish with parsley.

Nutritional Facts (Per Serving): Calories: 600 | Sugars: 6g | Fat: 25g | Carbohydrates: 40g | Protein: 30g | Fiber: 8g | Sodium: 700mg

Honey Garlic Chicken with Quinoa

Prep: 15 minutes | Cook: 4 hours | Serves: 6

Ingredients:

- 1.5 lbs boneless, skinless chicken thighs (680g)
- 1/3 cup honey (120g)
- 1/3 cup soy sauce (80ml)
- 3 cloves garlic, minced
- 1/4 cup ketchup (60ml)
- 1 tbsp olive oil
- 1 tsp dried basil
- 1 cup quinoa (170g)
- 2 cups chicken broth (500ml)
- Salt and pepper to taste
- 2 tbsp chopped fresh cilantro

Instructions:

1. Add chicken thighs, honey, soy sauce, garlic, ketchup, olive oil, and basil to the Crock Pot.
2. Cover and cook on low for 3 hours.
3. After 3 hours, add the rinsed quinoa and cook on high for an additional 1 hour until the quinoa is tender and has absorbed the liquid.
4. Serve chicken over quinoa and garnish with cilantro.

Nutritional Facts (Per Serving): Calories: 600 | Sugars: 8g | Fat: 25g | Carbohydrates: 35g | Protein: 30g | Fiber: 8g | Sodium: 700mg

Pork Tenderloin with Apples and Wild Rice

BBQ Pulled Chicken with Brown Rice

Prep: 15 minutes | Cook: 6 hours | Serves: 6

Prep: 15 minutes | Cook: 4 hours | Serves: 6

Ingredients:

- 1.5 lbs pork tenderloin (680g)
- 2 large apples, sliced (300g)
- 1 large onion, chopped (150g)
- 3 cloves garlic, minced
- 2 cups chicken broth (500ml)
- 1 cup wild rice (200g)
- 1/4 cup apple cider vinegar (60ml)
- 2 tbsp olive oil
- 1 tsp dried sage
- Salt and pepper to taste
- 2 tbsp chopped fresh parsley

Ingredients:

- 1.5 lbs boneless, skinless chicken breasts (680g)
- 1 cup BBQ sauce (240ml)
- 1 large onion, chopped (150g)
- 3 cloves garlic, minced
- 1/4 cup apple cider vinegar (60ml)
- 1 tbsp olive oil
- 1 tsp smoked paprika
- Salt and pepper to taste
- 2 cups cooked brown rice (370g)
- 2 tbsp chopped fresh cilantro

Instructions:

1. Add pork tenderloin, apples, onion, garlic, chicken broth, wild rice, apple cider vinegar, olive oil, sage, salt, and pepper to the Crock Pot.
2. Cover and cook on low for 6 hours.
3. Slice pork and serve with apples and wild rice. Garnish with parsley.

Instructions:

1. Add chicken breasts, BBQ sauce, onion, garlic, apple cider vinegar, olive oil, smoked paprika, salt, and pepper to the Crock Pot.
2. Cover and cook on low for 4 hours.
3. Shred the chicken with two forks and mix well with the sauce.
4. Serve over cooked brown rice and garnish with fresh cilantro.

Nutritional Facts (Per Serving): Calories: 600 | Sugars: 8g | Fat: 25g | Carbohydrates: 35g | Protein: 30g | Fiber: 8g | Sodium: 600mg

Nutritional Facts (Per Serving): Calories: 600 | Sugars: 8g | Fat: 25g | Carbohydrates: 40g | Protein: 30g | Fiber: 8g | Sodium: 600mg

Beef and Sweet Potato Shepherd's Pie

Prep: 20 minutes | Cook: 6 hours | Serves: 6

Ingredients:

- 1.5 lbs ground beef (680g)
- 1 large onion, chopped (150g)
- 3 cloves garlic, minced
- 2 cups beef broth (500ml)
- 2 cups diced carrots (300g)
- 1 cup peas (150g)
- 2 tbsp tomato paste
- 1 tbsp Worcestershire sauce
- 1 tsp dried thyme
- 1 tsp dried rosemary
- Salt and pepper to taste
- 3 cups mashed sweet potatoes (450g)
- 2 tbsp butter

Instructions:

1. Add ground beef, onion, garlic, beef broth, carrots, peas, tomato paste, Worcestershire sauce, thyme, rosemary, salt, and pepper to the Crock Pot.
2. Cover and cook on low for 6 hours.
3. Spread mashed sweet potatoes mixed with butter on top of the beef mixture before serving.

Nutritional Facts (Per Serving): Calories: 600 | Sugars: 8g | Fat: 25g | Carbohydrates: 35g | Protein: 30g | Fiber: 8g | Sodium: 600mg

Slow-Roasted Herb Chicken with Root Vegetables

Prep: 15 minutes | Cook: 6 hours | Serves: 6

Ingredients:

- 1 whole chicken (3.5 lbs/1.6kg)
- 1 large onion, quartered (150g)
- 3 cloves garlic, minced
- 2 cups chopped carrots (300g)
- 2 cups chopped parsnips (300g)
- 2 cups chopped potatoes (300g)
- 1/4 cup olive oil (60ml)
- 2 tbsp fresh rosemary, chopped
- 2 tbsp fresh thyme, chopped
- 1 tsp salt
- 1/2 tsp black pepper
- 1 lemon, halved

Instructions:

1. Rub the chicken with olive oil, rosemary, thyme, salt, and pepper.
2. Stuff the chicken with lemon halves and some of the onion.
3. Place remaining onion, garlic, carrots, parsnips, and potatoes in the Crock Pot.
4. Place the chicken on top of the vegetables.
5. Cover and cook on low for 6 hours.

Nutritional Facts (Per Serving): Calories: 600 | Sugars: 6g | Fat: 30g | Carbohydrates: 30g | Protein: 35g | Fiber: 7g | Sodium: 700mg

Italian Meatballs in Marinara Sauce with Orzo and Spinach

Prep: 20 minutes | Cook: 6 hours | Serves: 6

Ingredients:

- 1.5 lbs ground beef (680g)
- 1/2 cup breadcrumbs (60g)
- 1/4 cup grated Parmesan cheese (30g)
- 1 large egg, beaten
- 3 cloves garlic, minced
- 2 tbsp chopped fresh parsley
- 1 tsp dried oregano
- Salt and pepper to taste
- 4 cups marinara sauce (1 liter)
- 2 cups cooked orzo (350g)
- 4 cups fresh spinach (120g)

Instructions:

1. In a bowl, mix ground beef, breadcrumbs, Parmesan cheese, egg, garlic, parsley, oregano, salt, and pepper. Form into meatballs.
2. Place meatballs in the Crock Pot and cover with marinara sauce.
3. Cover and cook on low for 6 hours. Add the orzo 30 minutes before the end of cooking on high heat
4. Serve meatballs and sauce over cooked orzo, and stir in fresh spinach.

Nutritional Facts (Per Serving): Calories: 600 | Sugars: 8g | Fat: 25g | Carbohydrates: 35g | Protein: 35g | Fiber: 8g | Sodium: 700mg

Meatloaf with Mashed Cauliflower

Prep: 20 minutes | Cook: 6 hours | Serves: 6

Ingredients:

- 1.5 lbs ground beef (680g)
- 1/2 cup breadcrumbs (60g)
- 1/4 cup grated Parmesan cheese (30g)
- 1 large egg, beaten
- 1 large onion, finely chopped (150g)
- 3 cloves garlic, minced
- 2 tbsp ketchup
- 1 tsp dried thyme
- Salt and pepper to taste
- 1 large head cauliflower, chopped (600g)
- 1/4 cup heavy cream (60ml)
- 2 tbsp butter
- Salt and pepper to taste

Instructions:

1. In a bowl, mix ground beef, breadcrumbs, Parmesan cheese, egg, onion, garlic, ketchup, thyme, salt, and pepper. Form into a loaf.
2. Place meatloaf in the Crock Pot and cover.
3. Cook on low for 6 hours.
4. Boil cauliflower until tender, then drain. Mash with heavy cream, butter, salt, and pepper.
5. Serve meatloaf with mashed cauliflower.

Nutritional Facts (Per Serving): Calories: 600 | Sugars: 6g | Fat: 30g | Carbohydrates: 30g | Protein: 35g | Fiber: 8g | Sodium: 600mg

Beef and Vegetable Kebabs with Quinoa

Prep: 20 minutes | Cook: 4 hours | Serves: 6

Ingredients:

- 1.5 lbs beef sirloin, cubed (680g)
- 2 cups bell peppers, chopped (300g)
- 1 large onion, chopped (150g)
- 2 zucchinis, sliced (300g)
- 3 cloves garlic, minced
- 1/4 cup olive oil (60ml)
- 1/4 cup soy sauce (60ml)
- 2 tbsp balsamic vinegar
- 1 tsp dried oregano
- Salt and pepper to taste
- 1.5 cups quinoa, cooked (270g)
- 2 cups chicken broth (500ml)

Instructions:

1. In a bowl, combine beef, bell peppers, onion, zucchini, garlic, olive oil, soy sauce, balsamic vinegar, oregano, salt, and pepper.
2. Skewer the beef and vegetables alternately on kebab sticks.
3. Place kebabs in the Crock Pot and cover.
4. Cook on low for 4 hours.
5. Serve over cooked quinoa.

Nutritional Facts (Per Serving): Calories: 600 | Sugars: 6g | Fat: 25g | Carbohydrates: 35g | Protein: 35g | Fiber: 8g | Sodium: 700mg

Beef and Broccoli with Brown Rice

Prep: 15 minutes | Cook: 4 hours | Serves: 6

Ingredients:

- 1.5 lbs beef flank steak, sliced (680g)
- 4 cups broccoli florets (600g)
- 1 large onion, chopped (150g)
- 3 cloves garlic, minced
- 1/2 cup soy sauce (120ml)
- 1/4 cup beef broth (60ml)
- 1/4 cup honey (85g)
- 2 tbsp sesame oil
- 1 tbsp cornstarch
- 2 cups cooked brown rice (370g)
- 2 tbsp chopped green onions

Instructions:

1. In a bowl, combine beef, onion, garlic, soy sauce, beef broth, honey, and sesame oil.
2. Place mixture in the Crock Pot and cover.
3. Cook on low for 4 hours.
4. In the last 30 minutes, mix cornstarch with a bit of water and stir into the Crock Pot to thicken the sauce. Add broccoli florets.
5. Serve over cooked brown rice and garnish with green onions.

Nutritional Facts (Per Serving): Calories: 600 | Sugars: 8g | Fat: 20g | Carbohydrates: 40g | Protein: 35g | Fiber: 7g | Sodium: 800mg

CHAPTER 11: SNACKS: Healthy Snacks and Appetizers

Tomato Basil Bruschetta

Prep: 10 minutes | Cook: 2 hours | Serves: 4

Ingredients:

- 1 lb Roma tomatoes, diced (450g)
- 1/4 cup chopped fresh basil (10g)
- 2 tbsp olive oil (30ml)
- 1 tbsp balsamic vinegar (15ml)
- 2 cloves garlic, minced
- 1/2 tsp salt (2.5g)
- 1/4 tsp black pepper (1g)
- 1 baguette, sliced (about 200g)

Instructions:

1. In a bowl, combine tomatoes, basil, olive oil, balsamic vinegar, garlic, salt, and pepper.
2. Transfer the mixture to a Crock Pot.
3. Cook on low for 2 hours, stirring occasionally.
4. Toast baguette slices under a broiler until golden.
5. Top each slice with the tomato mixture and serve.

Nutritional Facts (Per Serving): Calories: 300 | Carbohydrates: 35g | Proteins: 10g | Fats: 12g | Fiber: 4g | Sodium: 380mg | Sugars: 5g

Greek Yogurt Spinach Dip with Veggie Sticks

Prep: 15 minutes | Cook: 2 hours | Serves: 4

Ingredients:

- 2 cups Greek yogurt (480g)
- 1 cup chopped fresh spinach (30g)
- 1/2 cup chopped scallions (50g)
- 2 cloves garlic, minced
- 1 tbsp olive oil (15ml)
- 1 tsp dried dill (2g)
- 1/2 tsp salt (2.5g)
- 1/4 tsp black pepper (1g)
- Assorted veggie sticks (carrots, celery, bell peppers) (300g)

Instructions:

1. Combine spinach, scallions, garlic, olive oil, dill, salt, and pepper in the Crock Pot.
2. Cook on low for 2 hours, stirring occasionally.
3. Remove from heat and stir in Greek yogurt until well combined.
4. Serve with veggie sticks.

Nutritional Facts (Per Serving): Calories: 300 | Carbohydrates: 30g | Proteins: 15g | Fats: 10g | Fiber: 4g | Sodium: 350mg | Sugars: 10g

Spinach Artichoke Dip with Whole Grain Lavash

Prep: 10 minutes | Cook: 2 hours | Serves: 4

Ingredients:

- 1 cup frozen spinach, thawed and drained (140g)
- 1 cup canned artichoke hearts, drained and chopped (240g)
- 1 cup Greek yogurt (240g)
- 1/2 cup grated Parmesan cheese (50g)
- 1/2 cup shredded mozzarella cheese (50g)
- 2 cloves garlic, minced
- 1 tbsp olive oil (15ml)
- 1/2 tsp salt (2.5g)
- 1/4 tsp black pepper (1g)
- 4 whole grain lavash pieces (200g)

Instructions:

1. Combine spinach, artichokes, Parmesan, mozzarella, garlic, olive oil, salt, and pepper in the Crock Pot.
2. Cook on low for 2 hours, stirring occasionally.
3. Remove from heat and stir in Greek yogurt until smooth.
4. Serve with lavash pieces.

Nutritional Facts (Per Serving): Calories: 300 | Carbohydrates: 35g | Proteins: 12g | Fats: 12g | Fiber: 4g | Sodium: 350mg | Sugars: 5g

Roasted Red Pepper Hummus with Pita

Prep: 10 minutes | Cook: 2 hours | Serves: 4

Ingredients:

- 1 can chickpeas, drained (15 oz / 425g)
- 1 roasted red pepper, chopped (150g)
- 1/4 cup tahini (60g)
- 2 tbsp lemon juice (30ml)
- 2 cloves garlic, minced
- 1 tbsp olive oil (15ml)
- 1/2 tsp salt (2.5g)
- 1/4 tsp cumin (1g)
- 4 whole wheat pita breads (200g)

Instructions:

1. Combine chickpeas, roasted red pepper, tahini, lemon juice, garlic, olive oil, salt, and cumin in a blender.
2. Blend until smooth.
3. Transfer to a Crock Pot and cook on low for 2 hours.
4. Serve with toasted pita breads.

Nutritional Facts (Per Serving): Calories: 300 | Carbohydrates: 35g | Proteins: 12g | Fats: 12g | Fiber: 5g | Sodium: 350mg | Sugars: 2g

Avocado and Black Bean Salsa with Tortilla Chips

Prep: 10 minutes | Cook: 2 hours | Serves: 4

Ingredients:

- 1 can black beans, drained and rinsed (15 oz / 425g)
- 1 avocado, diced (200g)
- 1 cup corn kernels (160g)
- 1/2 cup red onion, finely chopped (75g)
- 1/2 cup tomatoes, diced (75g)
- 1/4 cup cilantro, chopped (10g)
- 2 tbsp lime juice (30ml)
- 1 tbsp olive oil (15ml)
- 1/2 tsp salt (2.5g)
- 1/4 tsp black pepper (1g)
- 4 oz tortilla chips (120g)

Instructions:

1. Combine black beans, corn, red onion, tomatoes, cilantro, lime juice, olive oil, salt, and pepper in the Crock Pot.
2. Cook on low for 2 hours, stirring occasionally.
3. Remove from heat, gently fold in diced avocado.
4. Serve with tortilla chips.

Nutritional Facts (Per Serving): Calories: 300 | Carbohydrates: 35g | Proteins: 10g | Fats: 15g | Fiber: 5g | Sodium: 350mg | Sugars: 3g

Baked Brie with Berries

Prep: 10 minutes | Cook: 2 hours | Serves: 4

Ingredients:

- 8 oz wheel of brie cheese (225g)
- 1 cup mixed berries (150g)
- 2 tbsp honey (30ml)
- 1/4 cup chopped nuts (almonds or walnuts) (30g)
- 4 whole grain crackers (200g)

Instructions:

1. Place the brie cheese in the Crock Pot.
2. Top with mixed berries and honey.
3. Cook on low for 2 hours, until the cheese is melted and gooey.
4. Cheese Texture: Use a lid to retain moisture and prevent excessive bubbling.
5. Serve immediately to enjoy the gooey texture.

Nutritional Facts (Per Serving): Calories: 300 | Carbohydrates: 30g | Proteins: 12g | Fats: 15g | Fiber: 4g | Sodium: 300mg | Sugars: 10g

Baked Cinnamon Apples

Prep: 10 minutes | Cook: 2 hours | Serves: 4

Ingredients:

- 4 large apples, cored and sliced (800g)
- 1/4 cup low carb sweeteners (50g)
- 1 tsp ground cinnamon (2g)
- 1/4 cup water (60ml)
- 2 tbsp unsalted butter, melted (30g)

Instructions:

1. In a bowl, mix apple slices, low carb sweeteners, and cinnamon.
2. Place the mixture in the Crock Pot.
3. Pour water and melted butter over the apples.
4. Cook on low for 2 hours until apples are tender.
5. Variety: Add nuts or a sprinkle of vanilla extract for added flavor.
6. Consistency: Ensure apples are well-coated to prevent sticking.
7. Serve warm.

Nutritional Facts (Per Serving): Calories: 300 | Carbohydrates: 35g | Proteins: 1g | Fats: 12g | Fiber: 5g | Sodium: 100mg | Sugars: 15g

Lemon Blueberry Greek Yogurt Cake

Prep: 15 minutes | Cook: 3 hours | Serves: 4

Ingredients:

- 1 cup Greek yogurt (240g)
- 1 cup blueberries (150g)
- 1/2 cup low carb sweeteners (100g)
- 1/2 cup whole wheat flour (60g)
- 1/4 cup almond flour (30g)
- 2 large eggs
- 1 tsp baking powder (5g)
- Zest and juice of 1 lemon
- 1 tsp vanilla extract (5ml)

Instructions:

1. In a bowl, mix Greek yogurt, low carb sweeteners, eggs, lemon zest, lemon juice, and vanilla extract.
2. Add whole wheat flour, almond flour, and baking powder. Mix until well combined.
3. Prevent Sinking: Toss blueberries in a little flour before adding to prevent sinking.
4. Pour the batter into a greased Crock Pot.
5. Cook on low for 3 hours or until a toothpick comes out clean.
6. Cooling: Allow cake to cool in the Crock Pot for easier removal.

Nutritional Facts (Per Serving): Calories: 300 | Carbohydrates: 32g | Proteins: 12g | Fats: 12g | Fiber: 4g | Sodium: 150mg | Sugars: 10g

Lemon Chia Seed Pudding

Prep: 10 minutes | Cook: 2 hours | Serves: 4

Ingredients:

- 2 cups unsweetened almond milk (480ml)
- 1/2 cup chia seeds (80g)
- 1/4 cup low-carb sweeteners (50g)
- Zest and juice of 1 lemon
- 1 tsp vanilla extract (5ml)
- Fresh berries for topping (150g)

Instructions:

1. In a bowl, whisk together almond milk, chia seeds, low-carb sweeteners, lemon zest, lemon juice, and vanilla extract.
2. Transfer the mixture to the Crock Pot.
3. Prevent Sogginess: Place a trivet in the Crock Pot and set muffin cups on top to allow air circulation.
4. Cook on low for 2 hours, stirring occasionally.
5. Cooling: Allow muffins to cool slightly in the Crock Pot before removing to prevent sticking. Chill in the refrigerator for at least 1 hour before serving.
6. Top with fresh berries.

Nutritional Facts (Per Serving): Calories: 300 | Carbohydrates: 30g | Proteins: 10g | Fats: 15g | Fiber: 5g | Sodium: 150mg | Sugars: 10g

Peach Yogurt Crumble

Prep: 10 minutes | Cook: 2 hours | Serves: 4

Ingredients:

- 4 large peaches, sliced (800g)
- 1 cup Greek yogurt (240g)
- 1/2 cup low-carb sweeteners (100g)
- 1/2 cup rolled oats (50g)
- 1/4 cup almond flour (30g)
- 1/4 cup chopped almonds (30g)
- 2 tbsp unsalted butter, melted (30g)
- 1 tsp ground cinnamon (2g)

Instructions:

1. In a bowl, mix peaches and 1/4 cup low-carb sweeteners.
2. In another bowl, mix oats, almond flour, chopped almonds, melted butter, remaining sweeteners, and cinnamon.
3. Place peaches in the Crock Pot and spread the oat mixture on top.
4. Cook on low for 2 hours.
5. Serve warm with Greek yogurt.

Nutritional Facts (Per Serving): Calories: 300 | Carbohydrates: 35g | Proteins: 12g | Fats: 12g | Fiber: 5g | Sodium: 100mg | Sugars: 15g

Raspberry Almond Tart

Prep: 15 minutes | Cook: 3 hours | Serves: 4

Ingredients:

- 1 cup almond flour (120g)
- 1/4 cup low carb sweeteners (50g)
- 1/4 cup unsalted butter, melted (60g)
- 1 cup fresh raspberries (150g)
- 2 large eggs
- 1/2 cup Greek yogurt (120g)
- 1 tsp vanilla extract (5ml)
- 1/4 cup sliced almonds (30g)

Instructions:

1. Mix almond flour, low carb sweeteners, and melted butter to form a crust.
2. Press the crust mixture into the bottom of the Crock Pot.
3. In a bowl, whisk eggs, Greek yogurt, and vanilla extract.
4. Pour the egg mixture over the crust.
5. Top with fresh raspberries and sliced almonds.
6. Cook on low for 3 hours.
7. Let it cool before serving.

Nutritional Facts (Per Serving): Calories: 300 | Carbohydrates: 30g | Proteins: 12g | Fats: 15g | Fiber: 4g | Sodium: 150mg | Sugars: 10g

Vanilla Almond Protein Balls

Prep: 15 minutes | Cook: 2 hours | Serves: 4

Ingredients:

- 1 cup almond butter (240g)
- 1/2 cup low carb sweeteners (100g)
- 1/2 cup vanilla protein powder (60g)
- 1/4 cup almond flour (30g)
- 1/4 cup chopped almonds (30g)
- 2 tbsp chia seeds (30g)
- 1 tsp vanilla extract (5ml)

Instructions:

1. In a bowl, mix almond butter, low carb sweeteners, vanilla protein powder, almond flour, chopped almonds, chia seeds, and vanilla extract until well combined.
2. Roll the mixture into 1-inch balls.
3. Place the balls in the Crock Pot.
4. Cook on low for 2 hours.
5. Let them cool before serving.

Nutritional Facts (Per Serving): Calories: 300 | Carbohydrates: 30g | Proteins: 12g | Fats: 15g | Fiber: 5g | Sodium: 100mg | Sugars: 5g

Dark Chocolate Walnut Brownies

Prep: 15 minutes | Cook: 3 hours | Serves: 4

Ingredients:

- 1 cup almond flour (120g)
- 1/2 cup low carb sweeteners (100g)
- 1/2 cup unsweetened cocoa powder (50g)
- 1/4 cup unsalted butter, melted (60g)
- 1/4 cup chopped walnuts (30g)
- 2 large eggs
- 1 tsp vanilla extract (5ml)
- 1/2 tsp baking powder (2g)
- 1/4 tsp salt (1g)

Instructions:

1. In a bowl, mix almond flour, low carb sweeteners, cocoa powder, baking powder, and salt.
2. In another bowl, whisk melted butter, eggs, and vanilla extract.
3. Combine wet and dry ingredients, then fold in chopped walnuts.
4. Pour the batter into a greased Crock Pot.
5. Cook on low for 3 hours or until a toothpick comes out clean.
6. Let cool before serving.

Nutritional Facts (Per Serving): Calories: 300 | Carbohydrates: 30g | Proteins: 10g | Fats: 15g | Fiber: 5g | Sodium: 150mg | Sugars: 10g

Raspberry Oat Bars

Prep: 15 minutes | Cook: 2 hours | Serves: 4

Ingredients:

- 1 cup rolled oats (100g)
- 1/2 cup almond flour (60g)
- 1/2 cup low carb sweeteners (100g)
- 1/4 cup unsalted butter, melted (60g)
- 1 cup raspberry jam (250g)
- 1/4 cup chopped almonds (30g)
- 1 tsp vanilla extract (5ml)

Instructions:

1. In a bowl, mix rolled oats, almond flour, low carb sweeteners, and melted butter until crumbly.
2. Press half of the mixture into the bottom of a greased Crock Pot.
3. Spread raspberry jam evenly over the oat mixture.
4. Sprinkle the remaining oat mixture and chopped almonds on top.
5. Cook on low for 2 hours.
6. Let cool before cutting into bars.

Nutritional Facts (Per Serving): Calories: 300 | Carbohydrates: 35g | Proteins: 10g | Fats: 12g | Fiber: 5g | Sodium: 100mg | Sugars: 15g

CHAPTER 13: DESSERTS: Low-carb Baking Ideas

Blueberry Banana Bread

Prep: 15 minutes | Cook: 3 hours | Serves: 4

Ingredients:

- 2 ripe bananas, mashed (240g)
- 1 cup fresh blueberries (150g)
- 1 cup almond flour (120g)
- 1/2 cup low carb sweeteners (100g)
- 2 large eggs
- 1/4 cup unsalted butter, melted (60g)
- 1 tsp vanilla extract (5ml)
- 1 tsp baking powder (5g)
- 1/4 tsp salt (1g)

Instructions:

1. In a bowl, mix mashed bananas, eggs, melted butter, vanilla extract, and low carb sweeteners.
2. Add almond flour, baking powder, and salt, and mix until well combined.
3. Gently fold in fresh blueberries.
4. Pour the batter into a greased Crock Pot.
5. Cook on low for 3 hours or until a toothpick comes out clean.
6. Let cool before serving.

Nutritional Facts (Per Serving): Calories: 300 | Carbohydrates: 35g | Proteins: 10g | Fats: 12g | Fiber: 4g | Sodium: 150mg | Sugars: 15g

Lemon Poppy Seed Bread

Prep: 15 minutes | Cook: 3 hours | Serves: 4

Ingredients:

- 1 cup almond flour (120g)
- 1/2 cup coconut flour (60g)
- 1/2 cup low carb sweeteners (100g)
- 1/2 cup Greek yogurt (120g)
- 2 large eggs
- 1/4 cup unsalted butter, melted (60g)
- Zest and juice of 1 lemon
- 1 tbsp poppy seeds (10g)
- 1 tsp baking powder (5g)
- 1/4 tsp salt (1g)

Instructions:

1. In a bowl, mix almond flour, coconut flour, low carb sweeteners, baking powder, and salt.
2. In another bowl, whisk Greek yogurt, eggs, melted butter, lemon zest, and lemon juice.
3. Combine wet and dry ingredients, then fold in poppy seeds.
4. Pour the batter into a greased Crock Pot.
5. Cook on low for 3 hours or until a toothpick comes out clean.

Nutritional Facts (Per Serving): Calories: 300 | Carbohydrates: 32g | Proteins: 12g | Fats: 12g | Fiber: 4g | Sodium: 150mg | Sugars: 10g

Pumpkin Spice Bread

Prep: 15 minutes | Cook: 3 hours | Serves: 4

Ingredients:

- 1 cup almond flour (120g)
- 1/2 cup coconut flour (60g)
- 1/2 cup pumpkin puree (120g)
- 1/2 cup low carb sweeteners (100g)
- 2 large eggs
- 1/4 cup unsalted butter, melted (60g)
- 1 tsp pumpkin pie spice (5g)
- 1 tsp baking powder (5g)
- 1 tsp vanilla extract (5ml)
- 1/4 tsp salt (1g)

Instructions:

1. In a bowl, mix almond flour, coconut flour, low carb sweeteners, pumpkin pie spice, baking powder, and salt.
2. In another bowl, whisk pumpkin puree, eggs, melted butter, and vanilla extract.
3. Combine wet and dry ingredients.
4. Pour the batter into a greased Crock Pot.
5. Cook on low for 3 hours or until a toothpick comes out clean.
6. Allow to cool completely before removing to maintain structure.

Nutritional Facts (Per Serving): Calories: 300 | Carbohydrates: 32g | Proteins: 12g | Fats: 12g | Fiber: 4g | Sodium: 150mg | Sugars: 10g

Raspberry White Chocolate Bread

Prep: 15 minutes | Cook: 3 hours | Serves: 4

Ingredients:

- 1 cup almond flour (120g)
- 1/2 cup coconut flour (60g)
- 1/2 cup low carb sweeteners (100g)
- 1/2 cup Greek yogurt (120g)
- 2 large eggs
- 1/4 cup unsalted butter, melted (60g)
- 1 cup fresh raspberries (150g)
- 1/2 cup white chocolate chips (100g)
- 1 tsp baking powder (5g)
- 1/4 tsp salt (1g)
- 1 tsp vanilla extract (5ml)

Instructions:

1. In a bowl, mix almond flour, coconut flour, low carb sweeteners, baking powder, and salt.
2. In another bowl, whisk Greek yogurt, eggs, melted butter, and vanilla extract.
3. Combine wet and dry ingredients, then fold in raspberries and white chocolate chips.
4. Pour the batter into a greased Crock Pot.
5. Cook on low for 3 hours or until a toothpick comes out clean.
6. Prevent Sogginess: Use a trivet and place the baking dish on top to allow airflow.
7. Allow ample cooling time to set the bread properly.

Nutritional Facts (Per Serving): Calories: 300 | Carbohydrates: 35g | Proteins: 12g | Fats: 12g | Fiber: 4g | Sodium: 150mg | Sugars: 15g

Pecan Pie Bars

Prep: 15 minutes | Cook: 3 hours | Serves: 4

Ingredients:

- 1 cup almond flour (120g)
- 1/4 cup low carb sweeteners (50g)
- 1/4 cup unsalted butter, melted (60g)
- 1 cup pecans, chopped (100g)
- 1/2 cup low carb sweeteners (100g)
- 1/4 cup unsalted butter, melted (60g)
- 2 large eggs
- 1 tsp vanilla extract (5ml)
- 1/4 tsp salt (1g)

Instructions:

1. Mix almond flour, 1/4 cup low carb sweeteners, and 1/4 cup melted butter to form a crust.
2. Press the crust mixture into the bottom of the greased Crock Pot.
3. In another bowl, mix pecans, 1/2 cup low carb sweeteners, 1/4 cup melted butter, eggs, vanilla extract, and salt.
4. Pour the pecan mixture over the crust. Press crust firmly to prevent shifting during cooking.
5. Cook on low for 3 hours.
6. Let cool before cutting into bars.

Nutritional Facts (Per Serving): Calories: 300 | Carbohydrates: 30g | Proteins: 10g | Fats: 15g | Fiber: 4g | Sodium: 150mg | Sugars: 10g

Keto Bagels

Prep: 15 minutes | Cook: 2 hours | Serves: 4

Ingredients:

- 1 1/2 cups almond flour (180g)
- 1 tbsp baking powder (15g)
- 2 cups shredded mozzarella cheese (200g)
- 2 oz cream cheese (60g)
- 2 large eggs
- 1 tbsp sesame seeds (10g)

Instructions:

1. In a bowl, mix almond flour and baking powder.
2. Melt mozzarella and cream cheese together, then combine with the almond flour mixture.
3. Add eggs and knead until dough forms.
4. Divide dough into 4 parts and shape into bagels.
5. Line the Crock Pot with parchment paper or use a trivet to prevent bagels from sticking.
6. Place bagels in the Crock Pot and sprinkle with sesame seeds.
6. Cook on low for 2 hours. Rotate bagels halfway through cooking for even browning.
7. Let cool before serving.

Nutritional Facts (Per Serving): Calories: 300 | Carbohydrates: 32g | Proteins: 12g | Fats: 12g | Fiber: 4g | Sodium: 150mg | Sugars: 10g

Almond Butter Blondies

Prep: 15 minutes | Cook: 2 hours | Serves: 4

Ingredients:

- 1 cup almond butter (240g)
- 1/2 cup low carb sweeteners (100g)
- 1/4 cup almond flour (30g)
- 2 large eggs
- 1 tsp vanilla extract (5ml)
- 1/2 tsp baking powder (2g)
- 1/4 tsp salt (1g)

Instructions:

1. In a bowl, mix almond butter, low carb sweeteners, almond flour, eggs, vanilla extract, baking powder, and salt until well combined.
2. Pour the mixture into a greased Crock Pot.
3. Cook on low for 2 hours.
4. Let cool before cutting into blondies.

Nutritional Facts (Per Serving): Calories: 300 | Carbohydrates: 30g | Proteins: 12g | Fats: 15g | Fiber: 4g | Sodium: 150mg | Sugars: 10g

Cheddar Biscuits

Prep: 15 minutes | Cook: 2 hours | Serves: 4

Ingredients:

- 1 1/2 cups almond flour (180g)
- 1 cup shredded cheddar cheese (100g)
- 2 large eggs
- 2 tbsp unsalted butter, melted (30g)
- 1 tsp baking powder (5g)
- 1/4 tsp salt (1g)

Instructions:

1. In a bowl, mix almond flour, shredded cheddar cheese, baking powder, and salt.
2. In another bowl, whisk eggs and melted butter.
3. Combine wet and dry ingredients until a dough forms.
4. Drop spoonfuls of dough into the greased Crock Pot.
5. Cook on low for 2 hours or until biscuits are golden. Rotate biscuits halfway through cooking for even baking.
6. Let cool before serving.

Nutritional Facts (Per Serving): Calories: 300 | Carbohydrates: 32g | Proteins: 12g | Fats: 12g | Fiber: 4g | Sodium: 150mg | Sugars: 10g

Lemon Poppy Seed Muffins

Prep: 15 minutes | Cook: 2 hours | Serves: 4

Ingredients:

- 1 1/2 cups almond flour (180g)
- 1/4 cup low carb sweeteners (50g)
- 2 tbsp poppy seeds (20g)
- 2 large eggs
- 1/4 cup unsweetened almond milk (60ml)
- Zest and juice of 1 lemon
- 1 tsp baking powder (5g)
- 1/4 tsp salt (1g)

Instructions:

1. In a bowl, mix almond flour, low carb sweeteners, poppy seeds, baking powder, and salt.
2. In another bowl, whisk eggs, almond milk, lemon zest, and lemon juice.
3. Combine wet and dry ingredients until a batter forms.
4. Pour the batter into muffin cups and place in the Crock Pot. Place muffin cups on a trivet to allow air circulation.
5. Cook on low for 2 hours or until a toothpick comes out clean.
6. Let cool before serving.

Nutritional Facts (Per Serving): Calories: 300 | Carbohydrates: 35g | Proteins: 12g | Fats: 12g | Fiber: 4g | Sodium: 150mg | Sugars: 10g

Lemon Cheesecake

Prep: 20 minutes | Cook: 3 hours | Serves: 4

Ingredients:

- 2 cups almond flour (240g)
- 1/4 cup low carb sweeteners (50g)
- 1/2 cup unsalted butter, melted (120g)
- 16 oz cream cheese, softened (450g)
- 1/2 cup low carb sweeteners (100g)
- 2 large eggs
- Zest and juice of 1 lemon
- 1 tsp vanilla extract (5ml)

Instructions:

1. In a bowl, mix almond flour, 1/4 cup low carb sweeteners, and melted butter to form a crust.
2. Press the crust mixture into the bottom of a greased Crock Pot.
3. In another bowl, beat cream cheese, 1/2 cup low carb sweeteners, eggs, lemon zest, lemon juice, and vanilla extract until smooth.
4. Pour the cream cheese mixture over the crust. Smooth the top before cooking and avoid overcooking.
5. Cook on low for 3 hours or until set.
6. Allow cheesecake to cool completely to set properly.

Nutritional Facts (Per Serving): Calories: 300 | Carbohydrates: 30g | Proteins: 12g | Fats: 15g | Fiber: 4g | Sodium: 150mg | Sugars: 10g

Pineapple Upside Down Cake

Prep: 15 minutes | Cook: 3 hours | Serves: 4

Ingredients:

- 1/4 cup unsalted butter, melted (60g)
- 1/2 cup low carb sweeteners (100g)
- 1 can pineapple slices, drained (20 oz / 560g)
- 1/2 cup almond flour (60g)
- 1/2 cup coconut flour (60g)
- 1 tsp baking powder (5g)
- 1/4 tsp salt (1g)
- 1/2 cup Greek yogurt (120g)
- 2 large eggs
- 1 tsp vanilla extract (5ml)
- 1/4 cup pineapple juice (60ml)

Instructions:

1. Pour melted butter into the bottom of the greased Crock Pot.
2. Sprinkle 1/4 cup low carb sweeteners evenly over the butter.
3. Arrange pineapple slices on top.
4. In a bowl, mix almond flour, coconut flour, baking powder, salt, and remaining sweeteners.
5. In another bowl, whisk Greek yogurt, eggs, vanilla extract, and pineapple juice.
6. Combine wet and dry ingredients until a batter forms.
7. Pour the batter over the pineapple slices.
8. Cook on low for 3 hours or until a toothpick comes out clean.

Nutritional Facts (Per Serving): Calories: 300 | Carbohydrates: 35g | Proteins: 10g | Fats: 12g | Fiber: 4g | Sodium: 150mg | Sugars: 12g

Chocolate Lava Cake

Prep: 15 minutes | Cook: 2 hours | Serves: 4

Ingredients:

- 1/2 cup almond flour (60g)
- 1/2 cup unsweetened cocoa powder (50g)
- 1/2 cup low carb sweeteners (100g)
- 1/4 cup unsalted butter, melted (60g)
- 1/2 cup Greek yogurt (120g)
- 2 large eggs
- 1 tsp vanilla extract (5ml)
- 1/4 tsp salt (1g)
- 1/2 cup dark chocolate chips (80g)

Instructions:

1. In a bowl, mix almond flour, cocoa powder, low carb sweeteners, and salt.
2. In another bowl, whisk melted butter, Greek yogurt, eggs, and vanilla extract.
3. Combine wet and dry ingredients until smooth.
4. Fold in dark chocolate chips.
5. Pour the batter into greased ramekins and place in the Crock Pot.
6. Add 1 inch of water to the Crock Pot.
7. Cook on low for 2 hours or until the edges are set but the center is still gooey.
8. Let cool slightly before serving.

Nutritional Facts (Per Serving): Calories: 300 | Carbohydrates: 32g | Proteins: 12g | Fats: 15g | Fiber: 5g | Sodium: 150mg | Sugars: 12g

Caramel Apple Dump Cake

Prep: 15 minutes | Cook: 2 hours | Serves: 4

Ingredients:

- 4 large apples, peeled and sliced (800g)
- 1/2 cup low carb sweeteners (100g)
- 1 tsp ground cinnamon (2g)
- 1/2 cup unsalted butter, melted (120g)
- 1 cup almond flour (120g)
- 1/2 cup chopped pecans (60g)
- 1/4 cup sugar-free caramel sauce (60ml)

Instructions:

1. Place apple slices in the bottom of the greased Crock Pot.
2. Sprinkle low carb sweeteners and cinnamon over the apples.
3. Pour melted butter over the apples.
4. Top with almond flour and chopped pecans.
5. Drizzle sugar-free caramel sauce over the top.
6. Cook on low for 2 hours. Monitor apples to maintain texture.
7. Allow ample cooling time to set the layers properly.

Nutritional Facts (Per Serving): Calories: 300 | Carbohydrates: 35g | Proteins: 10g | Fats: 12g | Fiber: 5g | Sodium: 150mg | Sugars: 12g

Mango Coconut Rice Pudding

Prep: 15 minutes | Cook: 3 hours | Serves: 4

Ingredients:

- 1 cup Arborio rice (200g)
- 2 cups coconut milk (480ml)
- 1 cup water (240ml)
- 1/2 cup low carb sweeteners (100g)
- 1 ripe mango, diced (200g)
- 1 tsp vanilla extract (5ml)
- 1/4 tsp salt (1g)
- 1/4 cup shredded coconut (30g)

Instructions:

1. Combine Arborio rice, coconut milk, water, low carb sweeteners, vanilla extract, and salt in the Crock Pot. Stir gently to maintain rice texture.
2. Cook on low for 3 hours, stirring occasionally.
3. Add diced mango and shredded coconut in the last 30 minutes of cooking.
4. Let cool slightly before serving.

Nutritional Facts (Per Serving): Calories: 300 | Carbohydrates: 35g | Proteins: 10g | Fats: 12g | Fiber: 4g | Sodium: 150mg | Sugars: 10g

CHAPTER 14: DINNER:
Nutritious Sides and Vegetables

Ratatouille

Prep: 20 minutes | Cook: 4 hours | Serves: 4

Ingredients:

- 1 medium eggplant (300g), diced
- 2 medium zucchinis (400g), sliced
- 3 medium tomatoes (450g), chopped
- 1 red bell pepper (150g), chopped
- 1 yellow bell pepper (150g), chopped
- 1 can (15 oz) crushed tomatoes (425g)
- 1 large onion (150g), chopped
- 3 cloves garlic, minced
- 1 tsp dried thyme
- 1 tsp dried basil
- 2 tbsp olive oil (30ml)
- Salt and pepper to taste

Instructions:

1. Add eggplant, zucchinis, tomatoes, bell peppers, onion, and garlic to the Crock Pot.
2. Pour in the crushed tomatoes and olive oil.
3. Sprinkle with thyme, basil, salt, and pepper.
4. Stir to combine.
5. Cook on Low for 4 hours or until vegetables are tender.

Nutritional Facts (Per Serving): Calories: 350 | Sugars: 10g | Fat: 15g | Carbohydrates: 40g | Protein: 15g | Fiber: 6g | Sodium: 450mg

Vegetable Lasagna

Prep: 25 minutes | Cook: 4 hours | Serves: 6

Ingredients:

- 9 lasagna noodles (250g)
- 2 cups ricotta cheese (450g)
- 2 cups marinara sauce (500ml)
- 1 medium zucchini (200g), sliced
- 1 medium bell pepper (150g), chopped
- 1 cup spinach (30g), chopped
- 2 cups shredded mozzarella cheese (200g)
- 1 egg, beaten
- 2 tbsp grated Parmesan cheese (20g)
- Salt and pepper to taste

Instructions:

1. In a bowl, mix ricotta cheese, egg, spinach, salt, and pepper. Spread a thin layer of marinara sauce at the bottom of the Crock Pot. Layer 3 lasagna noodles, breaking to fit if necessary.
2. Spread 1/3 of the ricotta mixture over noodles. Add a layer of zucchini and bell pepper. Sprinkle 1/3 of the mozzarella cheese over vegetables.
3. Repeat layers twice, ending with mozzarella cheese. Sprinkle Parmesan cheese on top.
4. Cook on Low for 4 hours.

Nutritional Facts (Per Serving): Calories: 350 | Sugars: 8g | Fat: 15g | Carbohydrates: 35g | Protein: 20g | Fiber: 4g | Sodium: 500mg

Zucchini and Tomato Gratin

Prep: 15 minutes | Cook: 3 hours | Serves: 4

Ingredients:

- 2 medium zucchinis (400g), sliced
- 3 medium tomatoes (450g), sliced
- 1/2 cup grated Parmesan cheese (50g)
- 1/4 cup breadcrumbs (30g)
- 1/4 cup olive oil (60ml)
- 2 cloves garlic, minced
- 1 tsp dried oregano
- Salt and pepper to taste

Instructions:

1. Layer zucchini and tomato slices alternately in the Crock Pot.
2. In a small bowl, mix Parmesan cheese, breadcrumbs, garlic, oregano, salt, and pepper.
3. Sprinkle the cheese mixture over the vegetables.
4. Drizzle with olive oil.
5. Cook on Low for 3 hours or until vegetables are tender and top is golden.
6. For a crispier crust, add a little fresh cheese before serving.
7. Serve hot, garnished with fresh herbs.

Nutritional Facts (Per Serving): Calories: 350 | Sugars: 7g | Fat: 20g | Carbohydrates: 30g | Protein: 15g | Fiber: 5g | Sodium: 400mg

Savory Mushroom and Spinach Bake

Prep: 15 minutes | Cook: 3 hours | Serves: 4

Ingredients:

- 1 lb mushrooms (450g), sliced
- 6 cups fresh spinach (180g)
- 1 cup shredded mozzarella cheese (100g)
- 1 cup ricotta cheese (250g)
- 1/4 cup grated Parmesan cheese (25g)
- 1/2 cup low carb sweetener (100g)
- 2 cloves garlic, minced
- 2 tbsp olive oil (30ml)
- Salt and pepper to taste

Instructions:

1. Add mushrooms and spinach to the Crock Pot.
2. In a bowl, mix ricotta cheese, garlic, salt, and pepper.
3. Spread the ricotta mixture over the mushrooms and spinach.
4. Sprinkle mozzarella and Parmesan cheeses on top. Drizzle with olive oil.
5. Cook on Low for 3 hours or until the cheese is melted and bubbly.
6. For a creamier consistency, add a little cream or extra ricotta.
7. Serve hot, garnished with fresh herbs.

Nutritional Facts (Per Serving): Calories: 350 | Sugars: 6g | Fat: 20g | Carbohydrates: 30g | Protein: 18g | Fiber: 5g | Sodium: 450mg

Roasted Broccoli with Cauliflower and Cheese

Prep: 10 minutes | Cook: 2 hours | Serves: 4

Ingredients:

- 3 cups broccoli florets (300g)
- 3 cups cauliflower florets (300g)
- 1 cup shredded cheddar cheese (100g)
- 1/4 cup grated Parmesan cheese (25g)
- 1/4 cup olive oil (60ml)
- 1 tsp garlic powder
- Salt and pepper to taste

Instructions:

1. Add broccoli and cauliflower florets to the Crock Pot.
2. Drizzle with olive oil and sprinkle with garlic powder, salt, and pepper.
3. Toss to coat the vegetables evenly.
4. Sprinkle cheddar and Parmesan cheeses on top.
5. Cook on Low for 2 hours or until vegetables are tender and cheese is melted.
6. For a crispier texture, add some breadcrumbs or a little Parmesan 30 minutes before the end of cooking.
7. Serve hot, garnished with fresh herbs.

Nutritional Facts (Per Serving): Calories: 350 | Sugars: 4g | Fat: 20g | Carbohydrates: 35g | Protein: 18g | Fiber: 6g | Sodium: 400mg

Stuffed Mushrooms

Prep: 20 minutes | Cook: 2 hours | Serves: 4

Ingredients:

- 16 large mushrooms (400g), stems removed
- 1 cup breadcrumbs (120g)
- 1 cup shredded mozzarella cheese (100g)
- 1/2 cup grated Parmesan cheese (50g)
- 2 tbsp low carb sweetener (30g)
- 2 cloves garlic, minced
- 2 tbsp olive oil (30ml)
- 1 tsp dried oregano
- Salt and pepper to taste

Instructions:

1. Mix breadcrumbs, mozzarella cheese, Parmesan cheese, garlic, oregano, salt, and pepper in a bowl.
2. Stuff each mushroom cap with the cheese mixture.
3. Place stuffed mushrooms in the Crock Pot.
4. Drizzle with olive oil.
5. Cook on Low for 2 hours or until mushrooms are tender and filling is golden.
6. For a crispier texture, add some breadcrumbs or a little Parmesan 30 minutes before the end of cooking.
7. Serve hot, garnished with fresh herbs.

Nutritional Facts (Per Serving): Calories: 350 | Sugars: 5g | Fat: 18g | Carbohydrates: 35g | Protein: 20g | Fiber: 4g | Sodium: 450mg

CHAPTER 15: DINNER: Refreshing and Nutritious Salads

Warm Barley and Roasted Vegetable Salad

Prep: 15 minutes | Cook: 3 hours | Serves: 4

Ingredients:

- 1 cup barley (200g)
- 2 cups vegetable broth (480ml)
- 1 red bell pepper (150g), chopped
- 1 yellow bell pepper (150g), chopped
- 1 zucchini (200g), sliced
- 1 red onion (150g), chopped
- 2 tbsp olive oil (30ml)
- 1 tsp dried thyme
- Salt and pepper to taste

Instructions:

1. Add barley and vegetable broth to the Crock Pot.
2. Mix in bell peppers, zucchini, and red onion.
3. Drizzle with olive oil, and season with thyme, salt, and pepper.
4. Cook on Low for 3 hours or until barley is tender and vegetables are cooked.
5. For a richer flavor, add fresh herbs or nuts before serving. Serve warm, garnished with fresh herbs if desired.

Nutritional Facts (Per Serving): Calories: 350 | Sugars: 7g | Fat: 15g | Carbohydrates: 40g | Protein: 15g | Fiber: 6g | Sodium: 450mg

Black Bean and Corn Salad

Prep: 10 minutes | Cook: 2 hours | Serves: 4

Ingredients:

- 2 cups black beans (340g), cooked
- 1 cup corn kernels (160g)
- 1 red bell pepper (150g), chopped
- 1 green bell pepper (150g), chopped
- 1/4 cup fresh cilantro (15g), chopped
- 2 tbsp olive oil (30ml)
- 1 tbsp lime juice (15ml)
- 1 tsp cumin
- Salt and pepper to taste

Instructions:

1. Add black beans, corn, bell peppers, and cilantro to the Crock Pot.
2. Drizzle with olive oil and lime juice.
3. Sprinkle with cumin, salt, and pepper.
4. Stir to combine.
5. Cook on Low for 2 hours or until heated through.
6. For a fresher taste, add avocado before serving. Serve warm or at room temperature, garnished with fresh herbs.

Nutritional Facts (Per Serving): Calories: 350 | Sugars: 4g | Fat: 15g | Carbohydrates: 40g | Protein: 18g | Fiber: 6g | Sodium: 350mg

Warm Beet and Goat Cheese Salad

Prep: 15 minutes | Cook: 3 hours | Serves: 4

Ingredients:

- 4 medium beets (400g), peeled and chopped
- 1/4 cup goat cheese (60g), crumbled
- 2 tbsp balsamic vinegar (30ml)
- 2 tbsp olive oil (30ml)
- 1 tbsp honey (15g)
- 1/4 cup walnuts (30g), chopped
- Salt and pepper to taste

Instructions:

1. Add chopped beets to the Crock Pot.
2. Drizzle with olive oil and balsamic vinegar.
3. Add honey, salt, and pepper, and stir to coat the beets.
4. Cook on Low for 3 hours or until beets are tender.
5. Top with crumbled goat cheese and walnuts before serving. For extra flavor, you can add some fresh herbs or green onions.
6. Serve warm, garnished with fresh herbs.

Nutritional Facts (Per Serving): Calories: 350 | Sugars: 12g | Fat: 15g | Carbohydrates: 35g | Protein: 15g | Fiber: 5g | Sodium: 400mg

Spinach and Mushroom Salad with Balsamic Vinaigrette

Prep: 15 minutes | Cook: 2 hours | Serves: 4

Ingredients:

- 8 cups fresh spinach (240g)
- 1 lb mushrooms (450g), sliced
- 1/4 cup balsamic vinegar (60ml)
- 2 tbsp olive oil (30ml)
- 1 tbsp low carb sweetener (15g)
- 1 tsp Dijon mustard
- Salt and pepper to taste

Instructions:

1. Add sliced mushrooms to the Crock Pot.
2. In a bowl, whisk together balsamic vinegar, olive oil, low carb sweetener, Dijon mustard, salt, and pepper.
3. Pour the vinaigrette over the mushrooms and stir to coat.
4. Cook on Low for 2 hours or until mushrooms are tender.
5. Place fresh spinach in a serving bowl, top with warm mushrooms and vinaigrette.

Nutritional Facts (Per Serving): Calories: 350 | Sugars: 6g | Fat: 15g | Carbohydrates: 35g | Protein: 15g | Fiber: 6g | Sodium: 350mg

Quinoa and Kale Salad

Prep: 15 minutes | Cook: 2 hours | Serves: 4

Ingredients:

- 1 cup quinoa (170g), rinsed
- 2 cups vegetable broth (480ml)
- 4 cups chopped kale (120g)
- 1/4 cup lemon juice (60ml)
- 2 tbsp olive oil (30ml)
- 1 tbsp low carb sweetener (15g)
- 1 clove garlic, minced
- Salt and pepper to taste

Instructions:

1. Add quinoa and vegetable broth to the Crock Pot.
2. Cook on Low for 2 hours or until quinoa is tender.
3. In a bowl, whisk together lemon juice, olive oil, low carb sweetener, garlic, salt, and pepper.
4. Once quinoa is cooked, add chopped kale and lemon vinaigrette to the Crock Pot.
5. Stir well and let sit for 10 minutes before serving.

Nutritional Facts (Per Serving): Calories: 350 | Sugars: 4g | Fat: 15g | Carbohydrates: 40g | Protein: 15g | Fiber: 6g | Sodium: 400mg

Broccoli and Cranberry Salad

Prep: 15 minutes | Cook: 2 hours | Serves: 4

Ingredients:

- 4 cups broccoli florets (280g)
- 1/2 cup dried cranberries (60g)
- 1/2 cup plain Greek yogurt (120g)
- 2 tbsp low carb sweetener (30g)
- 1 tbsp apple cider vinegar (15ml)
- Salt and pepper to taste

Instructions:

1. Add broccoli florets to the Crock Pot.
2. In a bowl, mix Greek yogurt, low carb sweetener, apple cider vinegar, salt, and pepper.
3. Pour the yogurt dressing over the broccoli and stir to coat.
4. Cook on Low for 2 hours or until broccoli is tender.
5. Stir in dried cranberries before serving.

Nutritional Facts (Per Serving): Calories: 350 | Sugars: 10g | Fat: 15g | Carbohydrates: 35g | Protein: 20g | Fiber: 6g | Sodium: 300mg

Barley and Pomegranate Salad

Prep: 15 minutes | Cook: 3 hours | Serves: 4

Ingredients:

- 1 cup barley (200g)
- 2 cups vegetable broth (480ml)
- 1 cup pomegranate seeds (150g)
- 1/4 cup chopped fresh parsley (15g)
- 1/4 cup chopped fresh mint (15g)
- 2 tbsp olive oil (30ml)
- 2 tbsp lemon juice (30ml)
- Salt and pepper to taste

Instructions:

1. Add barley and vegetable broth to the Crock Pot.
2. Cook on Low for 3 hours or until barley is tender.
3. Once cooked, add pomegranate seeds, parsley, and mint.
4. Drizzle with olive oil and lemon juice.
5. Season with salt and pepper and stir to combine.

Nutritional Facts (Per Serving): Calories: 350 | Sugars: 10g | Fat: 15g | Carbohydrates: 40g | Protein: 15g | Fiber: 6g | Sodium: 150mg

Lentil and Feta Salad

Prep: 15 minutes | Cook: 2 hours | Serves: 4

Ingredients:

- 1 cup green lentils (200g), rinsed
- 2 cups water (480ml)
- 1 cup crumbled feta cheese (150g)
- 1/4 cup chopped red onion (35g)
- 1/4 cup chopped fresh parsley (15g)
- 2 tbsp red wine vinegar (30ml)
- 2 tbsp olive oil (30ml)
- 1 tsp dried oregano
- Salt and pepper to taste

Instructions:

1. Add lentils and water to the Crock Pot.
2. Cook on Low for 2 hours or until lentils are tender.
3. Drain any excess water.
4. Add crumbled feta, red onion, and parsley.
5. Drizzle with red wine vinegar and olive oil.
6. Season with oregano, salt, and pepper, then stir to combine.

Nutritional Facts (Per Serving): Calories: 350 | Sugars: 4g | Fat: 15g | Carbohydrates: 35g | Protein: 20g | Fiber: 6g | Sodium: 450mg

CHAPTER 16: DINNER: Fish and Seafood Delights

Lemon Garlic Salmon with Quinoa Pilaf

Prep: 15 minutes | Cook: 2 hours | Serves: 4

Ingredients:

- 4 salmon fillets (150g each)
- 1 cup quinoa (170g)
- 2 cups vegetable broth (480ml)
- 2 tbsp lemon juice (30ml)
- 2 cloves garlic, minced
- 2 tbsp olive oil (30ml)
- 1 tbsp chopped fresh dill (15g)
- Salt and pepper to taste

Instructions:

1. Add quinoa and vegetable broth to the Crock Pot.
2. Place salmon fillets on top of the quinoa.
3. In a small bowl, mix lemon juice, garlic, olive oil, dill, salt, and pepper.
4. Pour the lemon garlic mixture over the salmon.
5. Cook on Low for 2 hours or until salmon is tender and quinoa is cooked.

Nutritional Facts (Per Serving): Calories: 350 | Sugars: 2g | Fat: 15g | Carbohydrates: 30g | Protein: 25g | Fiber: 4g | Sodium: 300mg

Shrimp Scampi with Zucchini Noodles

Prep: 15 minutes | Cook: 1 hour | Serves: 4

Ingredients:

- 1 lb shrimp (450g), peeled and deveined
- 4 medium zucchinis (600g), spiralized into noodles
- 1/4 cup butter (60g)
- 2 tbsp olive oil (30ml)
- 4 cloves garlic, minced
- 1/4 cup lemon juice (60ml)
- 1 tsp red pepper flakes
- 1/4 cup fresh parsley (15g), chopped
- Salt and pepper to taste

Instructions:

1. Add butter, olive oil, and garlic to the Crock Pot.
2. Add shrimp, lemon juice, red pepper flakes, salt, and pepper.
3. Cook on Low for 1 hour or until shrimp is pink and cooked through.
4. Add zucchini noodles and cook for an additional 10 minutes until tender.
5. Stir in fresh parsley before serving.

Nutritional Facts (Per Serving): Calories: 350 | Sugars: 5g | Fat: 18g | Carbohydrates: 30g | Protein: 22g | Fiber: 5g | Sodium: 450mg

Mediterranean Cod with Couscous Salad

Prep: 15 minutes | Cook: 2 hours | Serves: 4

Ingredients:

- 4 cod fillets (600g)
- 1 cup couscous (170g)
- 1 cup vegetable broth (240ml)
- 1 cup cherry tomatoes (150g), halved
- 1/4 cup black olives (60g), sliced
- 2 tbsp capers (30g)
- 1/4 cup lemon juice (60ml)
- 2 tbsp olive oil (30ml)
- 1/4 cup fresh basil (15g), chopped
- Salt and pepper to taste

Instructions:

1. Place cod fillets in the Crock Pot.
2. Add cherry tomatoes, black olives, capers, lemon juice, olive oil, salt, and pepper.
3. Cook on Low for 2 hours or until cod is flaky and cooked through.
4. Prepare couscous according to package instructions using vegetable broth.
5. Mix cooked couscous with fresh basil and serve with the cod and vegetable mixture.

Nutritional Facts (Per Serving): Calories: 350 | Sugars: 6g | Fat: 15g | Carbohydrates: 35g | Protein: 25g | Fiber: 5g | Sodium: 400mg

Pesto Crusted Trout with Spinach and Cherry Tomatoes

Prep: 15 minutes | Cook: 2 hours | Serves: 4

Ingredients:

- 4 trout fillets (600g)
- 1/2 cup pesto (120g)
- 4 cups fresh spinach (120g)
- 1 cup cherry tomatoes (150g), halved
- 2 tbsp olive oil (30ml)
- 1/4 cup Parmesan cheese (25g), grated
- Salt and pepper to taste

Instructions:

1. Spread pesto evenly over trout fillets and place in the Crock Pot.
2. Add spinach and cherry tomatoes around the trout.
3. Drizzle with olive oil and sprinkle with Parmesan cheese, salt, and pepper.
4. Cook on Low for 2 hours or until trout is flaky and cooked through.

Nutritional Facts (Per Serving): Calories: 350 | Sugars: 4g | Fat: 20g | Carbohydrates: 30g | Protein: 20g | Fiber: 4g | Sodium: 450mg

Tilapia with Herb Butter and Roasted Asparagus

Prep: 15 minutes | Cook: 2 hours | Serves: 4

Ingredients:

- 4 tilapia fillets (600g)
- 1/4 cup butter (60g), softened
- 1 tbsp fresh parsley (15g), chopped
- 1 tsp fresh thyme (5g), chopped
- 1 tsp lemon zest (5g)
- 1 lb asparagus (450g), trimmed
- 2 tbsp olive oil (30ml)
- Salt and pepper to taste

Instructions:

1. In a small bowl, mix butter, parsley, thyme, and lemon zest.
2. Spread herb butter over tilapia fillets and place in the Crock Pot.
3. Add asparagus around the tilapia.
4. Drizzle asparagus with olive oil and season with salt and pepper.
5. Cook on Low for 2 hours or until tilapia is flaky and asparagus is tender.

Nutritional Facts (Per Serving): Calories: 350 | Sugars: 2g | Fat: 18g | Carbohydrates: 30g | Protein: 25g | Fiber: 5g | Sodium: 300mg

Spicy Cajun Catfish with Corn on the Cob

Prep: 15 minutes | Cook: 2 hours | Serves: 4

Ingredients:

- 4 catfish fillets (600g)
- 2 tbsp Cajun seasoning (30g)
- 4 ears corn on the cob (800g), halved
- 2 tbsp olive oil (30ml)
- 1 lemon (100g), sliced
- Salt and pepper to taste

Instructions:

1. Rub Cajun seasoning on both sides of catfish fillets and place in the Crock Pot.
2. Add halved corn on the cob around the catfish.
3. Drizzle olive oil over the corn and season with salt and pepper.
4. Top with lemon slices.
5. Cook on Low for 2 hours or until catfish is flaky and corn is tender.

Nutritional Facts (Per Serving): Calories: 350 | Sugars: 6g | Fat: 15g | Carbohydrates: 35g | Protein: 20g | Fiber: 5g | Sodium: 400mg

CHAPTER 17: DINNER: Family-Style Dinner Recipes

Chicken Pot Pie

Prep: 20 minutes | Cook: 4 hours | Serves: 4

Ingredients:

- 1 lb boneless, skinless chicken breasts (450g), cubed
- 2 cups mixed vegetables (peas, carrots, corn) (300g)
- 1 cup chicken broth (240ml)
- 1/2 cup heavy cream (120ml)
- 1/4 cup flour (30g)
- 1 onion (150g), chopped
- 2 cloves garlic, minced
- 1 tsp dried thyme
- 1 sheet puff pastry (230g), thawed
- 2 tbsp olive oil (30ml)
- Salt and pepper to taste

Instructions:

1. Add chicken, mixed vegetables, onion, garlic, chicken broth, heavy cream, flour, thyme, salt, and pepper to the Crock Pot.
2. Stir well to combine.
3. Cook on Low for 4 hours or until chicken is cooked through and mixture is thickened.
4. Preheat oven to 400°F (200°C), transfer the mixture to an oven-safe dish and top with pastry.
6. Bake in the preheated oven for 20 minutes.

Nutritional Facts (Per Serving): Calories: 350 | Sugars: 4g | Fat: 18g | Carbohydrates: 35g | Protein: 20g | Fiber: 4g | Sodium: 450mg

Farro and Roasted Vegetable Pilaf

Prep: 15 minutes | Cook: 3 hours | Serves: 4

Ingredients:

- 1 cup farro (200g)
- 2 cups vegetable broth (480ml)
- 1 red bell pepper (150g), chopped
- 1 zucchini (200g), chopped
- 1 cup cherry tomatoes (150g), halved
- 1 red onion (150g), chopped
- 2 tbsp olive oil (30ml)
- 1 tsp dried thyme
- Salt and pepper to taste

Instructions:

1. Add farro and vegetable broth to the Crock Pot.
2. Mix in red bell pepper, zucchini, cherry tomatoes, and red onion.
3. Drizzle with olive oil and season with thyme, salt, and pepper.
4. Cook on Low for 3 hours or until farro is tender.

Nutritional Facts (Per Serving): Calories: 350 | Sugars: 7g | Fat: 15g | Carbohydrates: 40g | Protein: 15g | Fiber: 6g | Sodium: 350mg

Beef and Bean Enchiladas

Prep: 20 minutes | Cook: 4 hours | Serves: 4

Ingredients:

- 1 lb ground beef (450g)
- 1 can black beans (15 oz) (425g), drained and rinsed
- 8 whole wheat tortillas (240g)
- 2 cups enchilada sauce (480ml)
- 1 cup shredded cheddar cheese (100g)
- 1 onion (150g), chopped
- 2 cloves garlic, minced
- 1 tsp chili powder
- 1 tsp cumin
- Salt and pepper to taste

Instructions:

1. Brown ground beef with onion and garlic in a skillet.
2. Add black beans, chili powder, cumin, salt, and pepper to the beef mixture.
3. Spoon the beef and bean mixture onto tortillas, roll them up, and place them seam-side down in the Crock Pot.
4. Pour enchilada sauce over the tortillas and sprinkle with cheddar cheese.
5. Cook on Low for 4 hours or until heated through and cheese is melted.

Nutritional Facts (Per Serving): Calories: 350 | Sugars: 6g | Fat: 15g | Carbohydrates: 35g | Protein: 25g | Fiber: 6g | Sodium: 400mg

Tomato Basil Zucchini Bake

Prep: 15 minutes | Cook: 2 hours | Serves: 4

Ingredients:

- 4 medium zucchinis (600g), sliced
- 2 cups diced tomatoes (400g)
- 1 cup shredded mozzarella cheese (100g)
- 1/4 cup grated Parmesan cheese (25g)
- 2 tbsp olive oil (30ml)
- 2 cloves garlic, minced
- 1/4 cup fresh basil (15g), chopped
- Salt and pepper to taste

Instructions:

1. Layer zucchini slices and diced tomatoes in the Crock Pot.
2. Drizzle with olive oil and add garlic, salt, and pepper.
3. Sprinkle with mozzarella and Parmesan cheeses.
4. Cook on Low for 2 hours or until zucchini is tender and cheese is melted. For a crispier crust, add some breadcrumbs or extra herbs 30 minutes before the end of cooking.
5. Top with fresh basil before serving.

Nutritional Facts (Per Serving): Calories: 350 | Sugars: 8g | Fat: 18g | Carbohydrates: 30g | Protein: 20g | Fiber: 5g | Sodium: 350mg

Mushroom and Spinach Lasagna

Prep: 20 minutes | Cook: 4 hours | Serves: 4

Ingredients:

- 9 lasagna noodles (250g)
- 2 cups ricotta cheese (450g)
- 2 cups shredded mozzarella cheese (200g)
- 2 cups fresh spinach (60g), chopped
- 2 cups mushrooms (300g), sliced
- 1 jar marinara sauce (24 oz) (680g)
- 1/4 cup grated Parmesan cheese (25g)
- 1 egg
- 2 cloves garlic, minced
- 2 tbsp olive oil (30ml)
- Salt and pepper to taste

Instructions:

1. In a bowl, mix ricotta cheese, egg, spinach, garlic, salt, and pepper.
2. Spread a thin layer of marinara sauce at the bottom of the Crock Pot.
3. Layer 3 lasagna noodles, breaking to fit if necessary.Spread 1/3 of the ricotta mixture over the noodles. Add a layer of sliced mushrooms and 1/3 of the mozzarella cheese.
4. Repeat layers twice, ending with mozzarella cheese on top. Sprinkle Parmesan cheese on top.
5. Cook on Low for 4 hours or until noodles are tender.

Nutritional Facts (Per Serving): Calories: 350 | Sugars: 10g | Fat: 18g | Carbohydrates: 35g | Protein: 20g | Fiber: 5g | Sodium: 450mg

Mushroom and Quinoa Stuffed Zucchini

Prep: 15 minutes | Cook: 2 hours | Serves: 4

Ingredients:

- 4 medium zucchinis (600g), halved and scooped out
- 1 cup quinoa (170g), cooked
- 1 cup mushrooms (150g), chopped
- 1/2 cup shredded mozzarella cheese (50g)
- 1/4 cup grated Parmesan cheese (25g)
- 2 cloves garlic, minced
- 2 tbsp olive oil (30ml)
- 1/4 cup fresh parsley (15g), chopped
- Salt and pepper to taste

Instructions:

1. In a bowl, mix cooked quinoa, mushrooms, garlic, parsley, salt, and pepper.
2. Stuff zucchini halves with the quinoa mixture.
3. Place stuffed zucchinis in the Crock Pot.
4. Drizzle with olive oil and sprinkle with mozzarella and Parmesan cheese.
5. Cook on Low for 2 hours or until zucchinis are tender. Add a little cheese 30 minutes before the end of cooking for a crispy crust.

Nutritional Facts (Per Serving): Calories: 350 | Sugars: 6g | Fat: 15g | Carbohydrates: 35g | Protein: 18g | Fiber: 5g | Sodium: 300mg

Classic Chicken and Vegetable Paella

Prep: 20 minutes | Cook: 4 hours | Serves: 4

Ingredients:

- 1 lb boneless, skinless chicken breasts (450g), cubed
- 1 cup Arborio rice (200g)
- 2 cups chicken broth (480ml)
- 1 red bell pepper (150g), chopped
- 1 green bell pepper (150g), chopped
- 1 cup green peas (150g)
- 1 onion (150g), chopped
- 2 cloves garlic, minced
- 1 tsp smoked paprika
- 1/2 tsp saffron threads
- 2 tbsp olive oil (30ml)
- Salt and pepper to taste

Instructions:

1. Heat olive oil in a skillet and brown the chicken cubes.
2. Transfer chicken to the Crock Pot.
3. Add Arborio rice, chicken broth, bell peppers, green peas, onion, garlic, smoked paprika, saffron, salt, and pepper.
4. Stir to combine.
5. Cook on Low for 4 hours or until rice is tender and liquid is absorbed.

Nutritional Facts (Per Serving): Calories: 350 | Sugars: 5g | Fat: 15g | Carbohydrates: 35g | Protein: 25g | Fiber: 4g | Sodium: 400mg

Mediterranean Turkey Paella

Prep: 20 minutes | Cook: 4 hours | Serves: 4

Ingredients:

- 1 lb ground turkey (450g)
- 1 cup Arborio rice (200g)
- 2 cups chicken broth (480ml)
- 1 red bell pepper (150g), chopped
- 1 green bell pepper (150g), chopped
- 1 cup cherry tomatoes (150g), halved
- 1 cup green peas (150g)
- 1 onion (150g), chopped
- 2 cloves garlic, minced
- 1 tsp smoked paprika
- 1/2 tsp saffron threads
- 2 tbsp olive oil (30ml)
- Salt and pepper to taste

Instructions:

1. Heat olive oil in a skillet and brown the ground turkey.
2. Transfer turkey to the Crock Pot.
3. Add Arborio rice, chicken broth, bell peppers, cherry tomatoes, green peas, onion, garlic, smoked paprika, saffron, salt, and pepper.
4. Stir to combine.
5. Cook on Low for 4 hours or until rice is tender and liquid is absorbed.

Nutritional Facts (Per Serving): Calories: 350 | Sugars: 6g | Fat: 15g | Carbohydrates: 35g | Protein: 25g | Fiber: 5g | Sodium: 450mg

Roasted Vegetable and Goat Cheese Tart

Prep: 15 minutes | Cook: 2 hours | Serves: 4

Ingredients:

- 1 sheet puff pastry (230g), thawed
- 1 red bell pepper (150g), chopped
- 1 zucchini (200g), sliced
- 1 cup cherry tomatoes (150g), halved
- 1/4 cup goat cheese (60g), crumbled
- 2 tbsp olive oil (30ml)
- 1 tsp dried thyme
- Salt and pepper to taste

Instructions:

1. Lay puff pastry in the Crock Pot.
2. Layer chopped red bell pepper, zucchini slices, and cherry tomatoes on the puff pastry.
3. Drizzle with olive oil and sprinkle with thyme, salt, and pepper.
4. Top with crumbled goat cheese.
5. Cook on Low for 2 hours or until vegetables are tender and pastry is cooked.

Nutritional Facts (Per Serving): Calories: 350 | Sugars: 7g | Fat: 20g | Carbohydrates: 30g | Protein: 15g | Fiber: 4g | Sodium: 300mg

Herbed Tomato and Feta Tart

Prep: 15 minutes | Cook: 2 hours | Serves: 4

Ingredients:

- 1 sheet puff pastry (230g), thawed
- 4 medium tomatoes (600g), sliced
- 1/2 cup crumbled feta cheese (75g)
- 2 tbsp olive oil (30ml)
- 1 tsp dried oregano
- 1 tsp dried basil
- Salt and pepper to taste

Instructions:

1. Lay puff pastry in the Crock Pot.
2. Arrange tomato slices over the puff pastry.
3. Drizzle with olive oil and sprinkle with oregano, basil, salt, and pepper.
4. Top with crumbled feta cheese.
5. Cook on Low for 2 hours or until tomatoes are tender and pastry is cooked.
6. Add some breadcrumbs or extra herbs 30 minutes before the end of cooking for a crispy crust.

Nutritional Facts (Per Serving): Calories: 350 | Sugars: 6g | Fat: 18g | Carbohydrates: 30g | Protein: 20g | Fiber: 5g | Sodium: 400mg

CHAPTER 18: BONUSES

Meal Plans and Shopping Templates

Simplify your Crock Pot Diet with our Ready-to-Use Meal Plans and Shopping Templates. Our 30-day grocery guide is crafted to complement this cookbook, emphasizing fresh, whole ingredients while minimizing processed foods. Be mindful of hidden sugars in sauces and dressings, and adjust quantities to suit your personal needs. Designed for one person, these templates streamline meal preparation, ensuring you enjoy nutritious and flavorful slow-cooked meals every day.

Grocery Shopping List for 7-Day Meal Plan

Meat & Poultry:

Beef stew meat – 1 lb / 450 g (Beef and Barley Stew)
Chicken breast (boneless, skinless) – 1 lb / 450 g (Chicken Noodle Soup, Chicken Pot Pie)
Ground turkey – 0.5 lb / 225 g (Turkey and Quinoa Chili)
Breakfast sausage – 0.5 lb / 225 g (Southwestern Egg and Sausage Breakfast Bake)
Bacon – 4 slices (Southwestern Egg and Sausage Breakfast Bake)
Chicken thighs – 0.5 lb / 225 g (Chicken Pot Pie)

Fish & Seafood:

Salmon fillet – 1 lb / 450 g (Lemon Garlic Salmon with Quinoa Pilaf)
Shrimp (peeled and deveined) – 0.5 lb / 225 g (Shrimp Scampi with Zucchini Noodles)
Cod fillet – 1 lb / 450 g (Mediterranean Cod with Couscous Salad)
Trout fillet – 1 lb / 450 g (Pesto Crusted Trout with Spinach and Cherry Tomatoes)
Tilapia fillet – 1 lb / 450 g (Tilapia with Herb Butter and Roasted Asparagus)
Catfish fillet – 1 lb / 450 g (Spicy Cajun Catfish with Corn on the Cob)

Vegetables:

Fresh spinach – 4 cups / 120 g (Spinach and Feta Egg Casserole, Savory Oatmeal with Spinach and Poached Egg, Spinach Artichoke Dip, Protein-Packed Veggie Omelette)
Mushrooms – 2 cups / 225 g (Cheesy Mushroom and Herb Frittata, Creamy Mushroom and Wild Rice Soup, Quiche Lorraine)
Tomatoes – 6 medium (Tomato Basil Bruschetta)
Cherry tomatoes – 2 pints / 680 g (Pesto Crusted Trout with Spinach and Cherry Tomatoes)
Red bell peppers – 2 medium (Beef and Barley Stew, Southwestern Egg and Sausage Breakfast Bake)
Zucchini – 4 medium (Zucchini and Parmesan Egg Muffins, Shrimp Scampi with Zucchini Noodles)
Onions – 4 large (Beef and Barley Stew, Chicken Noodle Soup, Vegetable Minestrone, Chicken Pot Pie)
Garlic – 2 bulbs (All recipes)
Carrots – 3 medium (Beef and Barley Stew, Vegetable Minestrone)
Celery – 2 stalks (Beef and Barley Stew, Chicken Noodle Soup)
Butternut squash – 1 small (Butternut Squash and Red Lentil Stew)
Broccoli – 1 large head (Creamy Broccoli and Cheddar Soup)
Asparagus – 1 bunch (Tilapia with Herb Butter and Roasted Asparagus)
Potatoes – 2 medium (Chicken Pot Pie)
Avocado – 1 medium (Avocado and Black Bean Salsa with Tortilla Chips)
Corn on the cob – 2 ears (Spicy Cajun Catfish with Corn on the Cob)

Fruits:

Apples – 2 medium (Baked Cinnamon Apples)
Mixed berries – 1 cup (Baked Brie with Berries)
Lemons – 3 medium (Lemon Garlic Salmon with Quinoa Pilaf, Shrimp Scampi with Zucchini Noodles, Pesto Crusted Trout with Spinach and Cherry Tomatoes)

Grains & Bread:

Quinoa – 1 cup / 180 g (Lemon Garlic Salmon with Quinoa Pilaf, Turkey and Quinoa Chili)
Barley – 1 cup / 200 g (Beef and Barley Stew)
Wild rice – 1 cup / 200 g (Creamy Mushroom and Wild Rice Soup)
Couscous – 1 cup / 180 g (Mediterranean Cod with Couscous Salad)
Whole grain lavash – 1 package (Spinach Artichoke Dip with Whole Grain Lavash)
Pita bread – 1 package (Roasted Red Pepper Hummus with Pita)
Tortilla chips – 1 bag (Avocado and Black Bean Salsa with Tortilla Chips)
Egg noodles – 8 oz / 225 g (Chicken Noodle Soup)
Bread (for Bruschetta) – 1 loaf (Tomato Basil Bruschetta)
Oats – 1/2 cup / 45 g (Savory Oatmeal with Spinach and Poached Egg)

Dairy & Eggs:

Eggs – 2 dozen (All recipes)

Feta cheese – 1 cup / 225 g (Spinach and Feta Egg Casserole, Spinach Artichoke Dip)
Parmesan cheese – 1/2 cup / 115 g (Savory Oatmeal with Spinach and Poached Egg, Pesto Crusted Trout with Spinach and Cherry Tomatoes)
Cheddar cheese – 1 cup / 225 g (Creamy Broccoli and Cheddar Soup)
Greek yogurt – 1 cup / 240 g (Greek Yogurt Spinach Dip)
Brie cheese – 4 oz / 115 g (Baked Brie with Berries)
Butter – 1 stick / 113 g (Tilapia with Herb Butter and Roasted Asparagus, Chicken Pot Pie)
Mozzarella cheese – 1 cup / 225 g (Pesto Crusted Trout with Spinach and Cherry Tomatoes)

Nuts, Seeds & Nut Butter:

Walnuts – 1/4 cup / 30 g (Optional for salads or toppings)
Almonds – 1/4 cup / 30 g (Optional for salads or toppings)
Chia seeds – 1/4 cup / 30 g (Optional for breakfast additions)

Pantry Staples:

Olive oil – 1 bottle
Vegetable or chicken broth – 6 cups / 1.5 L
Cooking spray or coconut oil – 1 can or bottle
Canned tomatoes – 1 can (Vegetable Minestrone)
Tomato paste – 1 small can
Soy sauce – 1 bottle (Shrimp Scampi with Zucchini Noodles)

Honey or maple syrup – 1 small bottle
Pesto sauce – 1 jar
Spices:
Salt
Black pepper
Thyme
Bay leaves
Cumin
Coriander
Paprika
Chili powder
Italian seasoning
Flour or cornstarch – 1 small bag
Hummus – 1 container (Roasted Red Pepper Hummus with Pita)
Tahini – 1 jar (Optional, for additional dips or dressings)

Herbs & Spices:

Fresh parsley – 1 bunch
Fresh cilantro – 1 bunch
Fresh thyme – 1 bunch
Fresh rosemary – 1 bunch
Fresh basil – 1 bunch

Grocery Shopping List for 8-14 Day Meal Plan

Meat & Poultry:

Beef stew meat – 1 lb / 450 g (Beef and Barley Stew, Beef and Bean Enchiladas, Beef and Sweet Potato Shepherd's Pie)
Chicken breast (boneless, skinless) – 1 lb / 450 g (Chicken and Vegetable Ragout, Chicken and Vegetable Paella)
Ground turkey – 0.5 lb / 225 g (Egg Muffins with Turkey and

Spinach, Turkey and Quinoa Chili)
Turkey sausage – 0.5 lb / 225 g (Turkey Sausage, Zucchini, and Egg White Casserole)
Bacon – 4 slices (Southwestern Egg and Sausage Breakfast Bake)
Chicken thighs – 0.5 lb / 225 g (Classic Chicken and Vegetable Paella)

Fish & Seafood:

Salmon fillet – 1 lb / 450 g (Broccoli, Cheddar, and Salmon Breakfast Quiche)
Shrimp (peeled and deveined) – 0.5 lb / 225 g (Shrimp Scampi with Zucchini Noodles)
Cod fillet – 1 lb / 450 g (Mediterranean Cod with Couscous Salad)
Trout fillet – 1 lb / 450 g (Pesto Crusted Trout with Spinach and Cherry Tomatoes)
Tilapia fillet – 1 lb / 450 g (Tilapia with Herb Butter and Roasted Asparagus)
Catfish fillet – 1 lb / 450 g (Spicy Cajun Catfish with Corn on the Cob)

Vegetables:

Fresh spinach – 6 cups / 180 g (Mushroom and Spinach Stuffed Peppers, Egg Muffins with Turkey and Spinach, Savory Oatmeal with Spinach and Poached Egg, Spinach and Ricotta Stuffed Shells)
Mushrooms – 3 cups / 340 g (Mushroom and Spinach Stuffed Peppers, Cheesy Mushroom and Herb Frittata, Creamy Mushroom and Wild

Rice Soup, Mushroom and Spinach Lasagna, Mushroom and Quinoa Stuffed Zucchini)
Tomatoes – 8 medium (Tomato Basil Bruschetta, Tomato Basil Zucchini Bake)
Cherry tomatoes – 1 pint / 340 g (Pesto Crusted Trout with Spinach and Cherry Tomatoes)
Red bell peppers – 3 medium (Mushroom and Spinach Stuffed Peppers, Beef and Bean Enchiladas, Grilled Vegetable and Hummus Wrap)
Zucchini – 6 medium (Egg Muffins with Turkey and Spinach, Tomato Basil Zucchini Bake, Mushroom and Quinoa Stuffed Zucchini, Grilled Vegetable and Hummus Wrap)
Onions – 6 large (Mushroom and Spinach Stuffed Peppers, Chicken and Vegetable Ragout, Beef and Bean Enchiladas, Broccoli, Cheddar, and Salmon Breakfast Quiche, Lentil and Vegetable Stew, Classic Chicken and Vegetable Paella)
Garlic – 4 bulbs (All recipes)
Carrots – 4 medium (Chicken and Vegetable Ragout, Lentil and Vegetable Stew)
Celery – 3 stalks (Chicken and Vegetable Ragout, Lentil and Vegetable Stew)
Butternut squash – 1 small (Butternut Squash and Red Lentil Stew)
Broccoli – 2 large heads (Broccoli, Cheddar, and Salmon Breakfast Quiche, Creamy Broccoli and Cheddar Soup)
Cauliflower – 1 medium head (Mushroom and Spinach Lasagna)

Asparagus – 1 bunch (Tilapia with Herb Butter and Roasted Asparagus)
Potatoes – 2 medium (Chicken and Vegetable Ragout, Classic Chicken and Vegetable Paella)
Avocado – 2 medium (Avocado and Black Bean Salsa with Tortilla Chips, Grilled Vegetable and Hummus Wrap)
Corn on the cob – 2 ears (Spicy Cajun Catfish with Corn on the Cob)
Cucumber – 1 large (Mediterranean Cod with Couscous Salad)
Artichoke hearts – 1 can or jar (Mediterranean Vegetable Ragout)
Mixed vegetables – 4 cups (Chicken and Vegetable Ragout, Classic Chicken and Vegetable Paella)

Fruits:

Apples – 2 medium (Farro and Apple Salad)
Blueberries – 1 cup (Lemon Blueberry Greek Yogurt Cake)
Mixed berries – 1 cup (Cottage Cheese and Raisin Berry Casserole)
Raspberries – 1 cup (Raspberry Almond Tart, Raspberry Oat Bars)
Peaches – 2 medium (Peach Yogurt Crumble)
Lemons – 4 medium (Lemon Blueberry Greek Yogurt Cake, Lemon Chia Seed Pudding, Tomato Basil Zucchini Bake)
Grains & Bread:
Quinoa – 2 cups / 360 g (Lemon Blueberry Greek Yogurt Cake, Quinoa and Black Bean

Salad, Mediterranean Turkey Paella)

Farro – 2 cups / 360 g (Farro and Roasted Vegetable Pilaf, Farro and Apple Salad)

Wild rice – 1 cup / 200 g (Wild Rice and Cranberry Salad)

Couscous – 1 cup / 180 g (Mediterranean Cod with Couscous Salad)

Lasagna noodles – 12 oz / 340 g (Mushroom and Spinach Lasagna, Spinach and Ricotta Stuffed Shells)

Whole grain tortillas – 1 package (Beef and Bean Enchiladas, Southwestern Egg and Sausage Breakfast Bake)

Whole grain lavash or pita bread – 1 package (Grilled Vegetable and Hummus Wrap)

Oats – 1 cup / 90 g (Peach Yogurt Crumble, Raspberry Oat Bars)

Egg noodles – 8 oz / 225 g (Beef and Bean Enchiladas)

Bread (for Bruschetta and Tart) – 1 loaf (Tomato Basil Bruschetta, Raspberry Almond Tart)

Dairy & Eggs:

Eggs – 2 dozen (All breakfast and casserole recipes)

Feta cheese – 1 cup / 225 g (Mushroom and Spinach Stuffed Peppers, Spinach and Ricotta Stuffed Shells)

Parmesan cheese – 1/2 cup / 115 g (Tomato Basil Zucchini Bake, Mushroom and Spinach Lasagna)

Cheddar cheese – 1 cup / 225 g (Broccoli, Cheddar, and Salmon Breakfast Quiche,

Creamy Broccoli and Cheddar Soup)

Greek yogurt – 2 cups / 480 g (Lemon Blueberry Greek Yogurt Cake, Greek Yogurt Spinach Dip)

Cottage cheese – 1 cup / 225 g (Cottage Cheese and Raisin Berry Casserole)

Butter – 1 stick / 113 g (Lemon Blueberry Greek Yogurt Cake, Dark Chocolate Walnut Brownies)

Mozzarella cheese – 1 cup / 225 g (Tomato Basil Zucchini Bake, Mushroom and Spinach Lasagna)

Ricotta cheese – 1 cup / 225 g (Spinach and Ricotta Stuffed Shells)

Nuts, Seeds & Nut Butter:

Walnuts – 1/2 cup / 75 g (Dark Chocolate Walnut Brownies, Cottage Cheese and Raisin Berry Casserole)

Almonds – 1/2 cup / 75 g (Raspberry Almond Tart, Vanilla Almond Protein Balls)

Chia seeds – 1/4 cup / 30 g (Lemon Chia Seed Pudding)

Pantry Staples:

Olive oil – 1 bottle

Vegetable or chicken broth – 6 cups / 1.5 L

Cooking spray or coconut oil – 1 can or bottle

Canned tomatoes – 2 cans (Mediterranean Vegetable Ragout, Lentil and Vegetable Stew)

Tomato paste – 1 small can (Beef and Bean Enchiladas)

Soy sauce – 1 bottle (Shrimp Scampi with Zucchini Noodles)

Honey or maple syrup – 1 small bottle (Lemon Blueberry Greek Yogurt Cake, Peach Yogurt Crumble)

Salt

Black pepper

Thyme

Bay leaves

Cumin

Coriander

Paprika

Chili powder

Italian seasoning

Cinnamon

Nutmeg

Vanilla extract

Flour or cornstarch – 1 small bag (Baking needs for cakes, tarts, and casseroles)

Hummus – 1 container (Grilled Vegetable and Hummus Wrap)

Tahini – 1 jar (Optional for additional dips or dressings)

Chickpeas – 1 can (Optional, for additional salads or dips)

Black beans – 2 cans (Beef and Bean Enchiladas, Quinoa and Black Bean Salad)

Kidney beans – 1 can (Beef and Bean Enchiladas)

Herbs & Spices:

Fresh parsley – 1 bunch (All recipes)

Fresh cilantro – 1 bunch (Quinoa and Black Bean Salad, Mediterranean Vegetable Ragout)

Fresh thyme – 1 bunch (Beef and Barley Stew, Chicken and Vegetable Ragout)

Fresh rosemary – 1 bunch (Classic Chicken and Vegetable Paella)

Fresh basil – 1 bunch (Tomato Basil Bruschetta, Tomato Basil Zucchini Bake)
Other:
Pesto sauce – 1 jar (Mushroom and Spinach Lasagna)
Whole grain lavash – 1 package (Grilled Vegetable and Hummus Wrap)

Meat & Poultry:

Beef stew meat – 1 lb / 450 g (Beef Stroganoff with Whole-Grain Noodles)
Pork tenderloin – 1 lb / 450 g (Pork Tenderloin with Apples and Wild Rice)
Chicken breast (boneless, skinless) – 1 lb / 450 g (Honey Garlic Chicken with Quinoa, BBQ Pulled Chicken with Brown Rice)
Ground turkey – 0.5 lb / 225 g (Egg Muffins with Turkey and Spinach)
Turkey sausage – 0.5 lb / 225 g (Turkey Sausage, Zucchini, and Egg White Casserole)
Bacon – 4 slices (Savory Amaranth with Bacon and Leeks, Savory Mushroom and Spinach Bake)

Vegetables:

Fresh spinach – 6 cups / 180 g (Spinach and Feta Egg Casserole, Egg Muffins with Turkey and Spinach, Savory Mushroom and Spinach Bake, Spinach and Feta Stuffed Peppers)
Mushrooms – 3 cups / 225 g (Mushroom and Spinach Stuffed Peppers, Savory Mushroom and Spinach Bake, Vegetable Lasagna)
Bell peppers – 3 medium (Spinach and Feta Egg Casserole, Spinach and Feta Stuffed Peppers)
Zucchini – 5 medium (Egg Muffins with Turkey and Spinach, Zucchini and Tomato Gratin, Vegetable Lasagna, Savory Mushroom and Spinach Bake)
Onions – 4 large (Spinach and Feta Egg Casserole, Egg Muffins with Turkey and Spinach, Creamy Tomato and Basil Pasta, Beef Stroganoff with Whole-Grain Noodles)
Garlic – 3 bulbs (All recipes)
Butternut squash – 1 small (Butternut Squash and Sage Risotto)
Leeks – 2 medium (Savory Amaranth with Bacon and Leeks)
Cauliflower – 1 medium head (Roasted Broccoli with Cauliflower and Cheese)
Broccoli – 1 large head (Broccoli, Cheddar, and Salmon Breakfast Quiche, Creamy Broccoli and Cheddar Soup, Roasted Broccoli with Cauliflower and Cheese)
Tomatoes – 6 medium (Creamy Tomato and Basil Pasta, Herbed Tomato and Feta Tart, Tomato Basil Zucchini Bake)
Cherry tomatoes – 1 pint / 340 g (Spinach and Feta Stuffed Peppers)
Pumpkin (fresh or canned) – 1 small can (Pumpkin Spice Bread)
Parsnips – 2 medium (Ratatouille)
Eggplant – 1 medium (Ratatouille)

Fruits:

Blueberries – 2 cups (Blueberry Banana Bread, Lemon Blueberry French Toast Casserole)
Bananas – 2 medium (Blueberry Banana Bread)
Pears – 2 medium (Gorgonzola and Pear Risotto)
Raspberries – 1 cup (Raspberry White Chocolate Bread, Raspberry Oat Bars)
Peaches – 2 medium (Peach Yogurt Crumble)
Lemons – 3 medium (Lemon Blueberry French Toast Casserole, Lemon Poppy Seed Bread, Lemon Blueberry Greek Yogurt Cake)
Apples – 2 medium (Pork Tenderloin with Apples and Wild Rice)
Mixed berries – 1 cup (Cottage Cheese and Raisin Berry Casserole)

Grains & Bread:

Quinoa – 1 cup / 180 g (Honey Garlic Chicken with Quinoa)
Farro – 1 cup / 180 g (Farro Breakfast Bowl with Roasted Vegetables)
Wild rice – 1 cup / 200 g (Pork Tenderloin with Apples and Wild Rice)

Couscous – 1 cup / 180 g (Mediterranean Cod with Couscous Salad)
Whole grain lasagna noodles – 12 oz / 340 g (Vegetable Lasagna)
Whole grain tortillas – 1 package (Beef and Bean Enchiladas)
Lavash bread or pita bread – 1 package (Grilled Vegetable and Hummus Wrap)
Bread (for tarts and casseroles) – 1 loaf (Roasted Vegetable and Goat Cheese Tart, Herbed Tomato and Feta Tart)
Banana bread mix or ingredients – Ingredients to make Blueberry Banana Bread (bananas, blueberries, flour, etc.)
Pumpkin bread ingredients – Ingredients to make Pumpkin Spice Bread
Pecan pie bar ingredients – Ingredients to make Pecan Pie Bars
Keto bagels – 4 (Keto Bagels)

Dairy & Eggs:

Eggs – 2 dozen (All breakfast and casserole recipes)
Feta cheese – 1 cup / 225 g (Spinach and Feta Egg Casserole, Spinach and Feta Stuffed Peppers)
Gorgonzola cheese – 1/2 cup / 115 g (Gorgonzola and Pear Risotto)
Parmesan cheese – 1 cup / 225 g (Creamy Tomato and Basil Pasta, Mushroom and Spinach Lasagna)
Cheddar cheese – 1 cup / 225 g (Broccoli, Cheddar, and Salmon Breakfast Quiche,
Creamy Broccoli and Cheddar Soup)
Goat cheese – 1/2 cup / 115 g (Roasted Vegetable and Goat Cheese Tart, Roasted Broccoli with Cauliflower and Cheese)
Greek yogurt – 2 cups / 480 g (Greek Yogurt Spinach Dip, Cottage Cheese and Raisin Berry Casserole)
Cottage cheese – 1 cup / 225 g (Cottage Cheese and Raisin Berry Casserole)
Butter – 1 stick / 113 g (Creamy Tomato and Basil Pasta, Roasted Broccoli with Cauliflower and Cheese)
Ricotta cheese – 1 cup / 225 g (Spinach and Ricotta Stuffed Shells)

Nuts, Seeds & Nut Butter:

Walnuts – 1/2 cup / 75 g (Raspberry White Chocolate Bread, Dark Chocolate Walnut Brownies)
Almonds – 1/2 cup / 75 g (Almond Butter Blondies, Raspberry Almond Tart)
Chia seeds – 1/4 cup / 30 g (Lemon Chia Seed Pudding)
Almond butter – 1/2 cup / 120 g (Almond Butter Blondies)
Pecans – 1/2 cup / 75 g (Pecan Pie Bars)
Pantry Staples:
Olive oil – 1 bottle
Vegetable or chicken broth – 6 cups / 1.5 L
Cooking spray or coconut oil – 1 can or bottle
Canned tomatoes – 2 cans (Mediterranean Vegetable Ragout, Lentil and Vegetable Stew)
Tomato paste – 1 small can (Creamy Tomato and Basil Pasta)
Soy sauce – 1 bottle (Various recipes)
Honey or maple syrup – 1 small bottle (Lemon Blueberry French Toast Casserole, Honey Garlic Chicken with Quinoa)
Spices:
Salt
Black pepper
Thyme
Bay leaves
Cumin
Coriander
Paprika
Chili powder
Italian seasoning
Cinnamon
Nutmeg
Vanilla extract
Sage (Butternut Squash and Sage Risotto)
Flour or cornstarch – 1 small bag (All baking recipes)
Hummus – 1 container (Grilled Vegetable and Hummus Wrap)
Tahini – 1 jar (Optional for additional dips or dressings)
Chickpeas – 1 can (Optional, for additional salads or dips)
Black beans – 2 cans (Beef and Bean Enchiladas, Quinoa and Black Bean Salad)
Kidney beans – 1 can (Beef and Bean Enchiladas)

Herbs & Spices:

Fresh parsley – 1 bunch (All recipes)
Fresh cilantro – 1 bunch (Quinoa and Black Bean Salad, Mediterranean Vegetable Ragout)
Fresh thyme – 1 bunch

Meat & Poultry:

Beef stew meat – 1 lb / 450 g (Beef and Sweet Potato Shepherd's Pie, Beef Stroganoff with Whole-Grain Noodles, Beef and Broccoli with Brown Rice, Beef and Vegetable Kebabs with Quinoa)
Ground beef or turkey – 1 lb / 450 g (Italian Meatballs in Marinara Sauce with Orzo, Beef and Bean Enchiladas)
Ground turkey – 0.5 lb / 225 g (Egg Muffins with Turkey and Spinach)
Chicken breast (boneless, skinless) – 1 lb / 450 g (Honey Garlic Chicken with Quinoa, Slow-Roasted Herb Chicken with Root Vegetables)
Chicken thighs – 1 lb / 450 g (Slow-Roasted Herb Chicken with Root Vegetables)
Turkey sausage – 0.5 lb / 225 g (Turkey Sausage, Zucchini, and Egg White Casserole)
Bacon – 4 slices (Savory Amaranth with Bacon and Leeks, Savory Mushroom and Spinach Bake)

Vegetables:

Fresh spinach – 8 cups / 240 g (Spinach and Feta Egg Casserole, Protein-Packed Veggie Omelette, Mushroom and Spinach Stuffed Peppers, Savory Oatmeal with Spinach and Poached Egg, Spinach and Mushroom Salad with Balsamic Vinaigrette)
Mushrooms – 4 cups / 450 g (Cheesy Mushroom and Herb Frittata, Stuffed Mushrooms, Cheesy Mushroom and Herb Frittata, Vegetable Lasagna)
Tomatoes – 8 medium (Creamy Tomato and Basil Pasta, Herbed Tomato and Feta Tart, Tomato Basil Zucchini Bake)
Cherry tomatoes – 2 pints / 680 g (Pesto Crusted Trout with Spinach and Cherry Tomatoes, Quinoa and Kale Salad)
Red bell peppers – 3 medium (Spinach and Feta Egg Casserole, Beef and Bean Enchiladas, Beef and Vegetable Kebabs with Quinoa)
Zucchini – 5 medium (Zucchini and Tomato Gratin, Vegetable Lasagna, Savory Oatmeal with Spinach and Poached Egg, Spinach and Feta Stuffed Peppers, Savory Mushroom and Spinach Bake)
Onions – 6 large (Spinach and Feta Egg Casserole, Beef and Sweet Potato Shepherd's Pie, Cheddar Biscuits, Beef Stroganoff with Whole-Grain Noodles, Slow-Roasted Herb Chicken with Root Vegetables)
Garlic – 4 bulbs (All recipes)
Butternut squash – 1 small (Butternut Squash and Sage Risotto)
Leeks – 2 medium (Savory Amaranth with Bacon and Leeks)
Cauliflower – 1 medium head (Broccoli and Cranberry Salad)
Broccoli – 2 large heads (Cheddar Biscuits, Broccoli and Cranberry Salad, Broccoli and Cheddar Soup)
Beets – 2 medium (Warm Beet and Goat Cheese Salad)
Eggplant – 1 medium (Eggplant Parmesan, Ratatouille)
Carrots – 3 medium (Beef and Sweet Potato Shepherd's Pie, Beef and Broccoli with Brown Rice, Beef and Sweet Potato Shepherd's Pie)
Celery – 2 stalks (Chicken and Vegetable Ragout, Lentil and Vegetable Stew)
Potatoes – 2 medium (Beef and Sweet Potato Shepherd's Pie, Zucchini and Tomato Gratin)

Fruits:

Blueberries – 2 cups (Blueberry Banana Bread, Lemon Blueberry French Toast Casserole)
Bananas – 2 medium (Blueberry Banana Bread)
Pears – 2 medium (Gorgonzola and Pear Risotto)
Raspberries – 1 cup (Raspberry White Chocolate Bread, Raspberry Oat Bars)
Peaches – 2 medium (Peach Yogurt Crumble)
Lemons – 4 medium (Lemon Poppy Seed Muffins, Lemon Cheesecake, Lemon Blueberry French Toast Casserole)
Apples – 2 medium (Beef and Sweet Potato Shepherd's Pie, Baked Cinnamon Apples)
Mixed berries – 1 cup (Cottage Cheese and Raisin Berry Casserole)
Mango – 1 medium (Mango Coconut Rice Pudding)
Grains & Bread:
Quinoa – 2 cups / 360 g (Honey Garlic Chicken with Quinoa, Beef and Vegetable Kebabs

with Quinoa, Quinoa and Black Bean Salad, Quinoa and Kale Salad)
Barley – 1 cup / 200 g (Warm Barley and Roasted Vegetable Salad)
Wild rice – 1 cup / 200 g (Pork Tenderloin with Apples and Wild Rice)
Couscous – 1 cup / 180 g (Eggplant Parmesan)
Whole grain lasagna noodles – 12 oz / 340 g (Vegetable Lasagna)
Orzo pasta – 1 cup / 180 g (Italian Meatballs in Marinara Sauce with Orzo and Spinach)
Whole grain tortillas – 1 package (Beef and Bean Enchiladas)
Lavash bread or pita bread – 1 package (Grilled Vegetable and Hummus Wrap)
Bread (for tarts and casseroles) – 1 loaf (Roasted Vegetable and Goat Cheese Tart, Herbed Tomato and Feta Tart)
Banana bread mix or ingredients – Ingredients to make Blueberry Banana Bread
Pumpkin bread ingredients – Ingredients to make Pumpkin Spice Bread
Pecan pie bar ingredients – Ingredients to make Pecan Pie Bars
Keto bagels – 4 (Keto Bagels)

Dairy & Eggs:

Eggs – 2 dozen (All breakfast and casserole recipes)
Feta cheese – 1.5 cups / 340 g (Spinach and Feta Egg Casserole, Spinach and Feta Stuffed Peppers)
Gorgonzola cheese – 0.5 cup / 115 g (Gorgonzola and Pear Risotto)
Parmesan cheese – 1.5 cups / 340 g (Cheddar Biscuits, Tomato Basil Zucchini Bake, Mushroom and Spinach Lasagna, Beef Stroganoff with Whole-Grain Noodles)
Cheddar cheese – 1.5 cups / 340 g (Cheddar Biscuits, Broccoli and Cheddar Soup)
Goat cheese – 0.5 cup / 115 g (Warm Beet and Goat Cheese Salad)
Greek yogurt – 2 cups / 480 g (Cottage Cheese and Raisin Berry Casserole, Greek Yogurt Spinach Dip)
Cottage cheese – 1 cup / 225 g (Cottage Cheese and Raisin Berry Casserole)
Butter – 1 stick / 113 g (Cheddar Biscuits, Baked Cinnamon Apples, Caramel Apple Dump Cake)
Ricotta cheese – 1 cup / 225 g (Spinach and Ricotta Stuffed Shells)

Mozzarella cheese – 1 cup / 225 g (Eggplant Parmesan, Zucchini and Tomato Gratin)
Nuts, Seeds & Nut Butter:
Walnuts – 1/2 cup / 75 g (Raspberry White Chocolate Bread, Cottage Cheese and Raisin Berry Casserole)
Almonds – 1/2 cup / 75 g (Almond Butter Blondies, Raspberry Almond Tart)
Chia seeds – 1/4 cup / 30 g (Lemon Chia Seed Pudding)
Almond butter – 1/2 cup / 120 g (Almond Butter Blondies)
Pecans – 1/2 cup / 75 g (Pecan Pie Bars)

Pantry Staples:

Olive oil – 1 bottle
Vegetable or chicken broth – 6 cups / 1.5 L
Cooking spray or coconut oil – 1 can or bottle
Canned tomatoes – 2 cans (Beef and Bean Enchiladas, Vegetable Minestrone, Lentil and Vegetable Stew)
Tomato paste – 1 small can (Italian Meatballs in Marinara Sauce with Orzo and Spinach)
Soy sauce – 1 bottle *(Savory Oatmeal with Spinach and Poached Egg,

Made in the USA
Las Vegas, NV
17 December 2024

14807708R00046